FRESH FROM MAINE

Recipes and Stories from the State's Best Chefs

FRESH FROM MAINE

Recipes and Stories from the State's Best Chefs

MICHAEL S. SANDERS

Photography By

RUSSELL FRENCH

table arts media

Published by Table Arts Media

Text Copyright © 2010 by Michael S. Sanders

Photographs © 2010 by Russell French

Cover and interior design by Lucian Burg of LuDesign

The text of this book is set in Frutiger

Printed in China by Elegance Printing

For information contact Table Arts Media, 46 Romasco Lane, Portland, Maine 04101.

ISBN-13: 978-0-9844775-0-0

The paper used in this publication meets the minimum requirements of the American National Standard for Information Services— Permanence of Paper for Printed Library Materials, ANSI/NISO Z39/48-1992

Preceding Title Page: Simmering Seafood Broth at Caiola's
Opposite: Hay Fields in Lincoln County

To my parents, who are my shining examples of love and dedication, and to Mary Anne and Eda, who keep me grounded with their love.

– Russell French

For Yves and Martine Jouffreau-Hermann, who shared their passion with me and who always encouraged me to be true to my own.

– Michael S. Sanders

Also by Michael S. Sanders

The Yard: Building a Destroyer at the Bath Iron Works

From Here, You Can't See Paris: Seasons of a French Village and Its Restaurant

Families of the Vines: Seasons Among the Winemakers of Southwest France

Acknowledgments

We would like to thank Lucian Burg of LuDesign for his endless enthusiasm about all things creative and vital to this project and food in general. Lucian has been a friend since the beginning. Along the way, we've been able to learn from each other, a great and ongoing conversation, generally over his great cooking.

We thank the chefs and owners, too, for jumping into the fire with us and trusting in us. We hope that you and your loyal clientele realize that your creativity and passion make our Maine communities stronger, more rewarding, a better place to live—and to eat. Particularly courageous were our first three converts, El, Daph, and Paul at El Camino, Sam at Fore Street, and Rob at Hugo's, and the Bar Harbor 3, as well, who signed on en masse. Various of you gave us a boost when we needed it along the way, fed us, re-arranged your lives to accommodate what was a furious schedule. We hope you see, in these pages, your best reflections in word and image which is truly how we see you.

Finally, it is hard to imagine that this fabulously rich world of Maine chefs and restaurants would exist without first the long and often unremarked work of the Maine Organic Farmers and Gardeners Association and its producer members. They blazed the trail that our many feet have followed, creating this movement towards a better, fairer, more sustainable, more ethical world. Support them.

Above: Slow-roasting Tomatoes at Cinque Terre
Opposite: Seagrass Bistro 3pm Prep

and more recipes . . .

Some dishes in this book are not accompanied by a recipe. You can find all of these recipes—and lots more about the chefs, their food, their thoughts—by going to **www.tableartsmedia.com**. Registration is free and easy.

Decadent Morel Mushrooms on Crisp Brioche at Solo Bistro

CONTENTS

"About 15 years ago, I began moving to incredibly simple preparations and presentations much more about the food itself than about the ideas I imposed on food. This is how I want to think of myself and Fore Street—as being part of a pure continuum that includes the raw production on the farm and the consumer at either end with me in the middle, performing a distillation but bringing those two ends around into a circle."

–Sam Hayward, Chef/Co-owner, Fore Street, Portland

Introduction

Maine is a land of surprises. It has a coastline longer than England's, more organic farms than California, and a terrifyingly short growing season of just 125 precious frost-free days. Making the most of what we can wrest from the soil or fish from the sea or forage from the woods, this is what Mainers have always done, a rich tradition that, today, feeds the state's vibrant and evolving food scene, from our farmers' markets to our dinner and restaurant tables.

Three forces have come together to launch Maine into the forefront of the good food movement. First, there are the producers, those hard-working men and women who are the local and organic movement's first responders, pioneers of everything from seed-saving to rare-breed husbandry to sustainable winter shrimping to resurrected estuarine clam, mussel, and oyster operations to innovative cheesemaking. They work their niches, from one end of the state to the other, inland to the Canadian border, and out into the Gulf of Maine.

Above: Truffled Lobster Mac 'n Cheese at five fifty five
Opposite: Pork rib racks and whole birds on the turnspit at Fore Street

Second, we have the chefs who are the passionate preachers of this new religion, happily as varied as their cuisines, each interpreting, innovating, reinventing as they serve themselves of the rich palette of flavors provided by Maine's diverse terroir.

Finally, there are what Slow Food founder Carlo Petrini calls "the co-producers". That's us, the consumers, who agree to support the producers and chefs for what they mean to our lives. Healthy food produced by our neighbors in an ethical way and sold at a fair price—and delicious!

Is it an accident that this triumvirate of forces has come together so significantly in Maine rather than, say, far wealthier Connecticut? I don't think so, for Maine is also an "edge" state, like Oregon or Idaho, all places of large area and little population and no metropolis, and consequently, all generally left to their own devices by the rest of the country which seems to race ever faster forward while we're still scraping the mud off our boots. That mud might be from the garden out back, or from the clam flats at low tide, or perhaps the woods, for Maine is also one of the most forested of all the states.

The good thing about being left alone and changing slowly is that, in this 21st century, our small corner of the country seems to have come to a startling realization: we have held on to more of our traditions, or, at least, have lost fewer, destroyed less landscape, and wiped out fewer ways of life in the rush to progress than most of our neighbors. Our traditional foods—heirloom vegetables, dried beans, apple varieties, and seafood dishes, even the ways we cook, whether the beanpot or Dutch oven or cast iron pan, these things have not been lost to the ages but here are experiencing a popularity that only grows each year.

I have lived in the same modest midcoast town for two decades now, and in that time have seen the arrival of bagels and baristas, a health foods store, and organic and all-natural food in the supermarket. More astoundingly, today, we can boast of three weekly outdoor farmers' markets, and one venue every Saturday morning in winter in an old mill space on the Androscoggin River. As I write this, you can buy there, among other things: free-range chickens and eggs, organic beef, pork, rabbit, and turkey, a rainbow of beets, turnips, potatoes, and other root vegetables, cheeses and yogurts, fresh-baked bread and pastry and pies, local roasted coffee, jams, pickles, and preserves. We have a lobsterman and clammer, a mussel gatherer, and a fisherman selling haddock, crab, Maine shrimp, and other Gulf of Maine fishes.

While what's available attests to the cleverness of our producers and the support of their customers, what impresses me is the warmth, the chatter, the buzz as a community comes together around its food at a time of year when the urge is to hibernate. My neighbors stamp the snow off their boots at the entrance, then pick up a cup of coffee and wander, reusable bags in hand, meeting friends, tasting, discussing their discoveries, pointing out a face new or old. There are mothers feeding babies, toddlers underfoot, and fiddlers sawing away in a far corner. It reminds me of every country market I have ever seen in France, Italy, Spain, Russia, Austria, and Hungary, markets that always used to make my wife and I wonder, on our return, why can't we have this at home? And now, at last, we do.

Above and Opposite: Fragrant Pine Needle Mussels at Francine Bistro

This being waning February, our northern state has just finished up its "trip around the dark side of the moon," as Steve Corry of five fifty five restaurant calls it poetically. This "trip" is that six-week period when the sun's rays hit the state so obliquely, when the temperature plunges so much, that no green thing will grow, no matter how gifted the four-season gardener. Chefs resign themselves to ever-more creative beet preparations, shaving the sweet Brussels sprouts, pulling out the last of the frozen tomato sauce and pickled summer vegetables against the day when Lisa of Laughing Stock or Martha from Farm Fresh or the New Leaf or Goranson folks or any of the other organic farmers calls with news of greens, blessed greens. And so the cycle begins again, with that sidewalk sandwich sign, the chalkboard hung over the bar, the e-mailed menu flash, all carrying the same joyous news that spring is here once again, and your favorite chef working her magic, keeping your table warm.

– Michael S. Sanders
February 2010, Brunswick, Maine

Southern Maine

Kittery to Portland

Above: Chef Charlie Cicero - Anneke Jans
Below: Chef Josh Mather - Joshua's Restaurant

Above: Chef Guy Hernandez - Bar Lola
Below: Chef Abby Harmon - Caiola's

Anneke Jans

Nestled into a weathered building on the main square of the oldest town in Maine, Anneke Jans has, in its dark wood bar, cozy interior, and homey welcome, much of the feel of a city neighborhood bistro.

"From the moment we opened in 2005," says Donna Ryan, co-owner with her partner, Andy Livingston, "we wanted to create a relaxed, friendly place that had a nice buzz. A place where after work executives in coat and tie feel as welcome as the table of six regulars in jeans and sports shirts sharing appetizers and joking with the waitperson. People seem to like eating at the bar as much as sitting at a table. Newcomers feel comfortable eating by themselves, and the regulars will introduce any new face to their neighbors."

From an open kitchen at the back of the room, Chef Charlie Cicero serves up his version of American bistro cuisine, dishes much influenced by the surrounding Atlantic waters and southern Maine farms. Andy Livingston's love of uncomplicated Mediterranean and southwestern French food still inspires the menu, "Country food, prepared simply," he says, "dishes without a lot of ingredients and served without heavy sauces, that's where we started out here. We've evolved. Charlie's put his own mark on the food, Donna, too. What Charlie does particularly well is cook fish, and that's an art in itself."

Chef Charlie Cicero

"I actually consider myself more of a cook than a chef," Cicero says, "because I am not someone who thinks the food has to be transformed from one thing into something else. Like sauces. A lot of food, if cooked properly, develops its own sauce whether you then just deglaze the pan or use the cooking juices. Whisk in a little butter . . ." He finishes, chuckling.

There are a few things on the menu that may surprise some customers, one of which is Livingston's original recipe for mussels with blue cheese. "It's a very simple dish," he says, "but its very unusual. People wonder if it's a mistake. In fact, it's one of our two or three most popular dishes. Then there's liver and onions. We sear the best calf's liver we can find, caramelize the onions, and add some bacon. We have some customers who come up from Boston once a month, just for the liver."

Every season has its own bounty and a signature dish or two. A rich cassoulet with house-made sausages and duck confit in darkest winter, or, as spring warms up, potato gnocchi with the first local peas and chanterelle mushrooms, lobster meat, and pickled pearl onions. "I pretty much ask myself," Chef Cicero says, "what would I like to eat right now with what's out there? And that's what we make."

Chef Cicero at a Glance

Where do you find inspiration?

Chef friends, eating out, reading the 400 cookbooks I own.

Do you have any chef heroes?

Chris Parsons at Catch Restaurant and Bradley Ogden in Vegas.

What do you like to do to relax?

Competitive barbecue. Hiking with my daughters.

Is there a spice mix or flavor profile you like?

I braise with thyme, but really salt and pepper—and lots of butter.

Is there a book that has recently inspired you?

John Thorne's *Serious Pig*, which I've read twice.

Do you have a favorite cheese?

Cabrales, from Spain, which is a very pungent blue.

Bangs Island Mussels with Great Hill Blue Cheese

Rinse the mussels, scrub the shells clean of grit, and pull the black beards off. Cut the bacon into ½" wide pieces, then cook it in a large sauté pan until crisp. Pour off all but about 1 tablespoon of the bacon fat. Sauté the shallots, garlic, salt, and pepper about 3 minutes in the fat until the shallots are browned then add white wine. Simmer until the wine is reduced by a third, then add all except 2 tablespoons of the blue cheese, cream, and mussels. Cook until mussels open. To serve, first discard any unopened mussels. Top the rest with the remaining 2 tablespoons crumbled blue cheese.

*Avoid most Chardonnays, as they can be too oaky and give the dish an off taste.

Serves 4

Ingredients

3 pounds Bangs Island mussels
1½ cups dry unoaked white wine*
¾ cup heavy cream
2 shallots, peeled and sliced thin
2 garlic cloves, peeled and minced
6-8 slices thick cut bacon
¾ cup Great Hill blue cheese, crumbled
Salt and pepper to taste

Bangs Island Mussels with Great Hill Blue Cheese

I pretty much ask myself, chef Cicero says, what would I like to eat right now with what's out there? And that's what we make.

The philosophy behind Anneke Jan's service is equally simple: be attentive, give the customers what they want, and encourage feedback. "We don't have any tricks here," says Anthony Aiken, who runs the front of the house. "Everyone is trained to pay attention to the customer. When your plate is set in front of you and you take that first bite, someone is paying attention."

"From the day we opened," Ryan adds, "we've asked our customers to tell us what they want and how they want it. We still get their feedback, and it helps us keep Anneke Jans a lively and fun place to eat."

Halibut with Polenta, Pancetta, Green Olives, and Tomato

First make the polenta: in a large, heavy-bottomed sauce pan, bring milk, olive oil, butter, salt and pepper to a boil. Reduce heat to low. Slowly whisk in polenta until thickened, 20-30 minutes. Check seasoning, adjust if necessary.

For the halibut: preheat oven to 350°F. Blanch, peel, and seed the tomatoes, then cut into ½" dice. Set aside. Slice the olives in half lengthwise. Set aside. Cut pancetta into strips ¼" wide and 1" long then cook over low heat until crisp, about 15 minutes. Drain and set aside. Place flour in large plate. Heat large sauté pan with 2 tablespoons of the olive oil. Season fish with salt and pepper then dredge 1 side only in the flour, shaking off excess. When pan is hot and oil is almost smoking, put the fish in it floured side down. Lower heat to medium, cook until golden brown, about 3-5 minutes. Remove pieces from pan and place on a baking sheet. Bake the fish in the oven 4-8 minutes depending on the thickness of the fish. In the sauté pan that was used for the fish, add pancetta, olives, and tomatoes. Season with salt and pepper. Heat until warm. Add lemon juice. Portion polenta onto four plates and top with pancetta mixture then the fish. Garnish with the finely chopped chives.

Serves 4

Ingredients
Polenta
3 cups milk
1-1½ cups Anson Mills polenta*
2 tablespoons butter
1 tablespoon extra virgin olive oil

Halibut
4 8-ounce East Coast halibut fillets
1 pound pancetta
16-20 large green Sicilian pitted olives
4-6 large tomatoes, blanched
Juice of 1 lemon
1 bunch chives, minced
3 tablespoons+ Wondra flour
2 tablespoons olive oil
Salt and pepper to taste

*If using box polenta, follow directions but substitute milk for water.

Maine Halibut with Anson Mills Polenta, Pancetta, Green Olives, and Tomato

Joshua's Restaurant

When you grow up in the 70's and 80's on a 100-acre farm with a huge organic garden, and your dad is one of the first presidents of MOFGA, and your mom bakes and sells a Fudge Pie famous from Portsmouth to Portland, is there any question but that your later life is going to somehow revolve around very good, very local food?

For Chef Josh Mather, who owns Joshua's Restaurant along with his mother, Barbara, and father, Mort, there was never any doubt. He worked his way up through the ranks at various restaurants on both coasts starting at age 14 as a lowly dishwasher. By age 27, he talked his way into his first executive chef post at Five-O in Ogunquit, leaving that to open his own place just two years later. Those early experiences provided a wealth of life lessons, too, from the very practical to the more esthetic.

Chef Josh Mather

"When I'd go with my dad on deliveries," Mather says, "we'd always go into the restaurant by the back door, through the kitchen. So I learned if you want something from a restaurant—to see the chef, ask for a job, sell them lettuce—you always go around back. Plus, I saw that kitchens were pretty cool, places where lots of action happened around stoves, flames, and people cutting things up with knives."

His parents, it turned out, had given him one gift whose importance it would take him some time to realize: a deep knowledge of and appreciation for the freshest garden vegetables and fruits, and of the flesh of the animals they raised on the farm, too, free-range chicken and natural pork and beef from their henhouse, wallows, and pastures.

"My education was first working in deep-fried restaurants." Mather says in his deadpan way. "I didn't go to culinary school. Then I ended up in Eugene, Oregon where I got hired on as a lunch chef and they told me to make the daily soup. I went to the library and got out Julia Child's **Mastering the Art of French Cooking** and started on page 1. Then I went in and made the soup the next day." From each chef he worked under, he would take what was good, squeezing the maximum out of the experience against the day when he could do what he wanted in his own place.

Today, Mather's cooking is in the best American tradition of incorporating ideas and techniques taken from other cultures but not letting them speak louder than the elemental ingredients, many of which will have had to travel that morning, from May to November, a scant half dozen miles from the family's farm. "A lot of my food comes from how I grew up, though it took me all that time working in other places to figure out how to make it work in a restaurant. Things like a slow roasted tomato or steamed beets, or maybe a side of parsnips, those are things Dad grew and Mom cooked."

In the idiom of Joshua's, the farm tomato's got an herb and homemade breadcrumb stuffing, the beets are slow-roasted then glazed with balsamic vinegar, and the parsnips are crunchy with a caramelized onion crust and meltingly soft on the inside. "But you can see what they are," Mather says emphatically, "taste what they are, really simple things just done well, which is what we do here."

Chef Mather at a Glance

Where do you find your inspiration?

From my mom, who gave me the roots of my cooking.

Do you have any chef heroes?

Tom Colicchio who wrote two great cookbooks, solid cookbooks.

Is there a book that has recently inspired you?

Peter Lynch's books about building wealth and investing.

Favorite late night snack?

Pan-fried fish with olive and anchovy sauce or maybe bread with honey.

What countries do you like to travel to?

France, especially Nice.

Do you have a favorite cheese?

Piave vecchio from the Veneto region in Italy.

Roasted Pepper Shrimp Sauté

Preheat 12" sauté pan. Put oil in pan, and when it is almost smoking, add shrimp, tomato, peppers, and garlic. Let cook for about 1 minute, then toss thoroughly just once to create a caramelized flavor. After 1 more minute, when the shrimp should be about half cooked, add the wine and salt to taste. Reduce the wine by half, cooking off the alcohol, then add the butter and parsley to finish. Serve immediately. We garnish this with a few pieces of grilled baguette, perfect for soaking up the sauce.

Serves 4 as an appetizer

Ingredients

3 tablespoons olive oil
1 pound white shrimp (21-25 count),
 peeled and deveined
1½ cups chopped tomato, in 1" dice
1 large roasted red pepper, thinly sliced
½ roasted jalapeño pepper, thinly sliced
2 tablespoons garlic, chopped
1 cup dry white wine
4 tablespoons unsalted butter
2 tablespoons fresh parsley, chopped
Salt to taste

Roasted Pepper Shrimp Sauté

Left: Chef Josh Mather
Below Right: Prepping Lamb Racks

Caramelized Onion Crusted Spice-Rubbed Rack of Lamb

For the rub: toast seeds in 350°F. oven for about 10 minutes. Remove from oven and cool. With a mortar and pestle, grind lightly, leaving some whole and some half crushed for varied flavor and texture. With a spoon, mix together mustard and seeds.

For the crust: heat a small, heavy-bottomed, high-sided sauce pan, add olive oil and onions. Cook on lowest stove setting, stirring occasionally, about 2 hours or until most of the moisture has evaporated and the onions are a deep amber color but not burnt. Cool in refrigerator. Put the bread crumbs into the bowl of a food processor and add the caramelized onion. Process until the crumbs stop falling back on themselves, about 1 minute. Crust is now ready to use, and will last a few days, or can be frozen.

For the lamb: preheat oven to 400°F. Remove the cap of fat and silvery skin from racks and cut each into 2 equal portions between the ribs. Salt both meat and bone sides of rack to taste. Rub mustard coriander mix on the meat and on the fatty part in between the bones but not on the bony underside. Press the caramelized onion crust into the meat. (It will stick to the wetter rub.)

Sear the lamb pieces one at a time before roasting all together. For each piece, put 2 tablespoons of olive oil in a frying pan and heat on high until almost smoking. Add lamb, crusted meat side down, pressing lightly to help create a thick, even crust which, after about 2 minutes, should be dark golden brown. (The crumbs that have fallen off are a good indicator as to how brown the crust is getting.) With a spatula, turn the rack so the bones are facing straight up, browning remaining crusted side for about 1 minute. Move, bony side down, to an oven-ready pan and roast 15-20 minutes, or until a meat thermometer inserted into thickest part registers 125°F for medium rare. Remove from oven, let racks rest about ten minutes, cut in-between each bone and serve immediately.

Serves 4 as an entrée

Ingredients

Mustard and Coriander Rub

½ cup smooth Dijon mustard
1½ teaspoons whole coriander seed
1½ teaspoons whole yellow mustard seed

Caramelized Onion Crust

2 cups fresh bread crumbs or
   Japanese panko
2 teaspoons olive oil
1 large yellow onion, about 2 cups,
   peeled and thinly sliced

Lamb

2 whole lamb racks, 4 ribs per person,
   about 2 pounds
4 tablespoons good quality olive oil
Salt

Caramelized Onion Crusted Spice-Rubbed Rack of Lamb

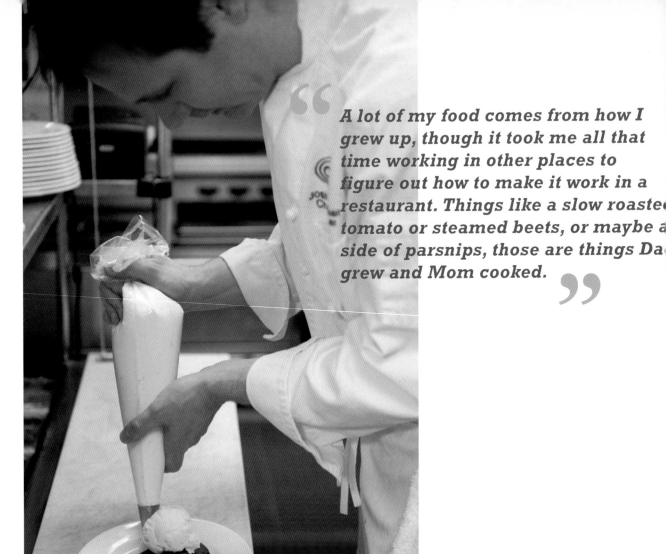

A lot of my food comes from how I grew up, though it took me all that time working in other places to figure out how to make it work in a restaurant. Things like a slow roasted tomato or steamed beets, or maybe a side of parsnips, those are things Dad grew and Mom cooked.

Chef Mather plating up dessert

When it came time to open Joshua's in 2004, he turned to his parents, whose personalities and abilities turned out to suit what was required very well indeed. "I work with my Dad on what he's going to grow every year." Mather explains. "All I have to say is, we need this, this much, at this time. Everything, particularly greens, loves our soil at the farm—butter lettuce and red leafs and Boston, mâche, lamb and corn lettuces, arugula. We make up our own salad mix, 4 or 5 months out of the year, it's 100% from our farm, then we turn to Lisa Turner at Laughing Stock Farm."

His mother is the hostess and runs the front of the house, but more importantly, Mather says honestly, "she's also my biggest supporter—and critic. She's the one who put together the dining rooms, the way they look and feel. She does all the flowers, the décor. Between her and my dad, we kind of make a complete whole. People come here and eat, and they get it, a family farm feeding a family restaurant that feeds them."

Barbara Mather's Sinfully Good Fudge Pie

Pre-heat oven to 350°F. Melt the butter. Use a double boiler to melt the chocolate. Using the whip attachment, in the bowl of a mixer infuse the sugar with the hot melted butter on high speed. Reduce speed to low and begin to add the flour and eggs a bit at a time, then the melted chocolate and vanilla extract, until all ingredients are just incorporated. (If mixed too long, the result is more cakelike when baked.) Pour mixture into a 9" glass pie plate. Bake in the oven 35 minutes.

You can garnish this with fresh berries or a fruit coulis. We love to serve it with a scoop of homemade vanilla ice cream and a dollop of whipped cream, then drizzle it with crème de menthe.

Serves 8-10

Ingredients

10 ounces lightly salted butter
2 cups granulated sugar
4 eggs
1⅓ cups all-purpose flour
4 ounces unsweetened chocolate
2 teaspoons pure vanilla extract

Barbara Mather's Sinfully Good Fudge Pie

Bar Lola

Ask Guy Hernandez what kind of food he serves at Bar Lola, the 34-seat restaurant he and his wife, Stella, opened in 2006 on Munjoy Hill, and he is likely to smile and answer, "Yes." One look at the 25-item menu of small, medium, and large plates and you understand that he's not being facetious, but honest, for what stitches

the food together is not a country or region or palette of ingredients, but instead an approach and a purpose. Both Stella and Guy were trained as architects, and the same compelling interplay of functionality and art in that profession turns up in their food, extending even to how Stella runs the front of the house.

Guy began cooking seriously under the tutelage of Allison Reid and Josh Potocki at One-Fifty-Ate in South Portland, where they quickly nicknamed him "the Mathemagician" because of his penchant for creating flow charts and yield graphs to better control the complicated baking formulas and processes there. When the restaurant added a full dinner service, it was only natural for Guy to evolve along with it, broadening his skills. "I'm interested in rigorous technique," he notes, "but

Chef Guy Hernandez

I'm also totally fine making it up as I go. So when I bake, I weigh everything."

"But he's also not afraid to take a risk, like the time he roasted an enormous whole red snapper for a private event where there would be no second chance to get it right." Stella remarks.

Consider one small plate, the sardines on crackers with hot sauce. "It's not that we made our own hot sauce or our own crackers or that the sardines are the finest line-caught Portuguese sardines you can get." Guy says, though this is true. "It is that all of these things have been pared down and done properly. This is what a cracker should taste like and a real sardine with just the right heat and that these three elements come together in this one dish, this one bite, this one plate, and that's it, you can't take anything else away. It's enough."

> " . . . this interweaving of taste and a gentle hand guiding your experience at the table through layers of richness and flavors and juxtapositions of things hot and cold, salt and sweet, bitter and earthy . . . "

Chef Hernandez at a Glance

Do you have a spice mixture or flavor profile that pleases you?

Filipino adobo, a soy and vinegar braise with bay and garlic, always reminds me of my father.

Favorite midnight snack?

A fried egg sandwich with hot sauce and mayonnaise.

What's your favorite cheese?

Autumn Oak, a raw sheep's milk from Willow Hill Farm in Vermont.

Do you have a book that recently inspired you?

John Thorne's *Serious Pig*, David Chang's *Momofuku*.

Do you have a favorite country to travel to?

Spain, France, and the Basque regions, those are high on our list.

Crispy Mortadella and Egg on Toasted Brioche with Mornay

Preheat oven to 350°F. **Mornay sauce:** bring milk to simmer in saucepan and add onion, bay leaf, cloves, and chili flakes. Let steep off the heat for 15 minutes. Strain and season to taste with salt and pepper. Melt 2 tablespoons butter in 2-quart, heavy-bottom saucepan. Sprinkle in flour and cook over low heat, stirring constantly for 2-3 minutes. Take pan off the heat and slowly add milk, whisking until smooth. Cook over medium low heat until thick enough to coat the back of a wooden spoon. Remove from heat and stir in cheese, whisking until smooth. Set aside.

Heat large oven-proof skillet over medium high heat and add 2 tablespoons of butter. When butter is melted, add brioche slices. Cook for two minutes on the stove top, place 1 tablespoon Mornay sauce on each slice and finish toasting in preheated oven.

Egg and mortadella: heat another skillet over medium high heat. Melt 2 tablespoons butter in pan and add eggs. Season with salt and pepper. Cook on stovetop until whites begin to set, about 2 minutes. Finish cooking in oven until whites are just set, another 3-4 minutes. While brioche is toasting and eggs are cooking, trim mortadella slices to roughly size of toasts and fry in pan over medium high heat until crispy.

To serve, place a 1 tablespoon of Mornay sauce on each of 4 warm plates, then a brioche slice, then top each slice with mortadella, the egg, and a garnish of chopped chives.

Serves 4

Ingredients

2 cups whole milk
½ Spanish onion, cut into thick wedges
1 bay leaf
2 whole cloves
1 teaspoon chili flakes
Salt and pepper
2 tablespoons butter
2 tablespoons flour
½ cup grated Swiss cheese
4 slices of brioche, crusts removed
4 thick slices quality mortadella
4 fresh farm eggs
4 tablespoons butter
1-2 tablespoons freshly chopped chives

Crispy Mortadella on Toasted Brioche with Mornay Sauce and a Fried Egg

"And just when you're thinking, was that really enough," Stella adds, "another plate arrives, taking you in a completely different direction and before you know it, you've had a 5 or 7 course meal with some plates as familiar as an old family recipe and others that may be at the edge or even just outside your comfort zone."

She mentions a past menu item, a cured octopus salad. "If you've never had it, " she says, "would you risk paying $18 to try something you're totally unfamiliar with? Probably not. But for $5 would you be willing to trust us and try it and discover something new? Sure."

And that is where the art comes in, in this interweaving of taste and a gentle hand guiding your experience at the table through layers of richness and flavors and juxtapositions of things hot and cold, salt and sweet, bitter and earthy, not too much and not too little, in a casual place that's precise but where there's never a question of which fork to use.

"We like what we do, we have a lot of fun," Stella finishes, "and we hope it shows."

Above: Chicken with Saffron Noodles

Pan-Roasted Striped Bass with Endive and Orange

Peel away any brown outer leaves from each endive. Cut in half lengthwise and then cut a wedge out of the bottom of each half to remove the core. Do not separate the leaves. Season with salt and freshly ground pepper. Heat oil in deep sauté pan large enough to hold endive in a single layer. Add endive halves, and brown on all sides. Add orange slices, tarragon, wine, and enough stock to cover. Gently simmer for 20 minutes. Remove endive and keep warm. Discard orange slices and tarragon and reduce cooking liquid by half. Reduce heat to low and whisk in butter, 1 tablespoon at a time. Season to taste with salt and pepper and add parsley, chives, and tarragon. Keep warm on low until serving.

Dry fish fillets and season both sides generously with salt and freshly ground pepper. Heat oil over medium heat in pan large enough to comfortably hold all fillets, or work in batches. Add fillets, skin side down and cook 4-5 minutes. Carefully flip over, add butter and thyme and cook the rest of the way through, about another 3-4 minutes, basting with the melted butter. Divide endive and sauce between 4 warm plates and top each with a fish fillet.

Serves 4

Ingredients

Endive and Orange Garnish

8 Belgian endives
2 tablespoons olive oil
Salt and pepper
1 cup dry white wine
3 cups fish or vegetable stock
1 orange, cut into ⅛" wedges, seeds removed
1 sprig fresh tarragon
8 tablespoons unsalted butter
1 tablespoon fresh flat leaf parsley, chopped
1 tablespoon chives, chopped
1 tablespoon fresh tarragon, chopped

Fish

4 fillets of striped bass, skin on (about 2 lbs.)
2 tablespoons olive oil
Salt and pepper
2 tablespoons butter
2 sprigs of fresh thyme

Pan-Roasted Striped Bass with Endive and Orange

Caiola's

After 14 years at Street & Co. where she finished up as Executive Chef, Abby Harmon packed up a van and headed out to travel the country for a year with her partner, Lisa Vaccaro. Except that a persistent friend wouldn't stop calling, filling their ears with news of a North End jewel box of a space for *their* restaurant, which the two had already decided to name after Lisa's grandmother, Caiola.

"Abby went in," Lisa recalls, laughing, "and she went right up to this beautiful old cork and wood door, the door to the walk-in. 'I want this place,' she said. Didn't look at the space. Didn't think how many seats or where does the bar go."

"I knew you could do the structural stuff, the kitchen." Abby replies with a shrug. "That's why we're a good team."

And right there, you have pretty much the essence of what makes Caiola's so much more than just a comfy, reasonably-priced, neighborhood joint with great fish just one part of an accomplished, unpretentious menu—though it is all of those things, too. Abby, from Cutler, almost as far downeast as you can go, brings a deep and real connection to rural seacoast New England cooking and traditions, amply influenced by European travel and Italian dinners around the table of her partner's extended family.

Chef Abby Harmon

"I love being in New England," she says, "because you can take all the fish here but cook it like you were in Sicily or France or Spain, with those flavors, using those techniques and ideas. Like the Sicilian Sardine Pasta I make. I was raised on sardines, my mom packed sardines in a factory downeast, and it's just been a part of my life. But now add Sicily, where they'll throw in fennel, currants, pine nuts . . ." She finishes, almost smacking her lips.

Lisa, an artist and cabinetmaker, is responsible for the just-so surroundings, all terracotta floors and barn board tables and trim, which together with the comfort food, give Caiola's a groove more pub than formal restaurant. "Abby gets to be creative in the kitchen," she says, "but I get to be creative out here." She gestures at the space, which includes an intimate nook right when you walk in, then an open foyer and bar, to the right and rear two other areas with tables tucked behind half walls because, she continues, "I wanted to make sure every table was next to a wall. It's more comfortable and private for people, I think, or they can eat at the bar if they want company."

Finnan haddie, cod brandade, beef tongue, and grilled sardines—all of these you'll find on the menu, for Abby is faithful to the food of her youth. "My uncle had whole sides of butterflied salt cod hanging from his porch," she remembers, "and finnan haddie you ate with an egg sauce. My mom would make New England boiled dinner, but with salt cod in place of the corned beef and plenty of beets, carrots, potatoes, and cabbage."

Chef Harmon at a Glance

Where do you find your inspiration?

Through my travels, in books from cooks like Elizabeth David and Julia Child and Richard Olney.

Do you have a spice or a flavor that particularly pleases you?

Anchovies, as a flavor base slow-cooked in their own oil plus olive oil and garlic until they get really nutty and the fish flavor disappears.

Do you have any chef heroes?

Paul Bertolli is someone whose life I've loved watching unfold, particularly after Chez Panisse.

Favorite midnight snack?

Canned fish. Anything pickled. I love things with vinegar and salt.

Is there a book that has influenced you lately?

Falling Cloudberries: A World of Family Recipes by Tessa Kiros.

Brandade with Oil-cured Olives, Orange, and Crostini

For the brandade: soak salt cod for 48 hours in cold water, changing water morning and night. Put the cod in a pan, cover with cold water. Bring to a boil then reduce to simmer, until fish flakes lightly, about 20-25 minutes depending on the thickness. Remove from pan with slotted spoon, pat dry, cover, and reserve. In the same pot and water, cook the potatoes until fork tender, drain, then rice or mash, preferably the former. Using a Cuisinart, pulse the salt cod a few times, keeping some of it in bigger flakes for texture. Heat 1 tablespoon olive oil in small sauté pan, add leek and cook until soft. Remove leek with slotted spoon and reserve, add ¼ cup olive oil to the same pan, and heat gently. Heat ¼ cup of heavy cream in another small saucepan. In a large mixing bowl gently combine puréed salt cod with mashed potatoes, reserved leek, and minced garlic. Begin adding hot cream and oil a little at a time, and check seasoning of purée, adding black pepper if desired.

To serve: preheat oven to 350°F. Cut the baguettes into ¼" slices on the bias, toss with 2 tablespoons olive oil, season with salt and pepper. Bake on a sheet pan until crisp and golden. Set aside. Place brandade in a baking dish, and pour as much remaining cream on top as you want. Create peaks on top of dish using the tines of a fork. Bake until brown, bubbling, and hot in the center, about 10-15 minutes. Garnish brandade with a little orange zest, oil cured olives, and the crostini on the side. A crisp white wine or dry rosé accompanying the brandade will complement its garlicky richness.

Serves 4-5 as an appetizer

Ingredients

- 1½ pounds salt cod
- ¼ cup+3 tablespoons extra virgin olive oil
- ½ cup heavy cream
- 2-3 cloves of garlic, cleaned and minced
- 1½-2 pounds Yukon Gold potatoes, washed and peeled
- 1 leek, white part only, cleaned and sliced fine
- ¼ pound oil-cured black olives, pitted
- Zest of ½ orange

ndade with Oil-cured Olives, Orange, and Crostini

"I love being in New England," she says, "because you can take all the fish here but cook it like you were in Sicily or France or Spain, with those flavors, using those techniques and ideas. Like the Sicilian Sardine Pasta I make. I was raised on sardines, my mom packed sardines in a factory downeast, and it's just been a part of my life. But now add Sicily, where they'll throw in fennel, currants, pine nuts . . ."

Above: Pan Sautéing Sardines with Fresh Rosemary
Below: Sicilian Sardine Pasta with Fennel, Pine Nuts, and Orange Zest

Grilled Calamari with White Bean & Spinach Salad

For the calamari marinade: combine the tamari, orange juice, garlic, honey, and pepper in a large bowl. Add the calamari, and marinate for 2 hours, refrigerated.

For the bean and spinach salad: clean and dry spinach. Drain beans, rinse with cold water, and set aside. Toss the spinach in olive oil and season.

For the calamari: heat a large stovetop grill pan brushed with canola oil very hot—almost smoking. Place drained calamari on the grill with seasoned spinach and cook until both are slightly charred, about 3 minutes. In a large bowl, toss the calamari with the white beans, charred spinach, vinegar, lime juice, capers, orange, and season with additional salt if necessary. Portion onto 4 plates and serve.

Note: using frozen calamari results in smaller portions as the thawed product shrinks when cooked.

Serves 4 as an appetizer

Ingredients:

Squid and Marinade

2 pounds calamari, in ¼" rings
¼ cup of tamari or soy sauce
¼ cup orange juice
2 cloves garlic, minced
2 tablespoons honey
1 tablespoon crushed red pepper (optional)
Canola oil

Salad

3 cups spinach, rinsed and dried
1 15-ounce ounce can Cento or Pastene cannellini beans
1 tablespoon olive oil
1 tablespoon red wine vinegar
Juice of 1 lime
1 tablespoon capers
1 orange, pith removed and sectioned
Salt

Grilled Calamari with White Bean & Spinach Salad

Abby and Lisa, however, in melding the cultures and cuisines of their two families in Caiola's dishes, are neither rigid nor outrageous, instead occupying a happy middle ground. You can see this in the appetizers, a remarkable array of varied plates, nearly two-thirds under $10, catering to the tastes and wallets of their diverse neighborhood and giving the chefs a free hand to create. "It's affordable, and delicious," Abby says, "and it keeps us true to our local farms and fishermen, not cutting any corners on ingredients, but being smart. It also allows us to have a truly collaborative kitchen, where we're always learning from each other." You may not find turbot garnished with caviar, in other words, but that Sicilian Sardine pasta with toasted fennel, pine nuts, and orange zest ain't too shabby.

The restaurant is ever-evolving, too, with Caiola's having added a Sunday brunch "that brings in a younger, professional crowd to try our food," Lisa says, "who then decide to come back for dinner." Recently, they opened the renovated back room, adding another 25 seats to the 35 up front, as well as a terrace in season. Their version of an "open" kitchen is two stained glass panels set into the wide doors of the kitchen. Created specially for the space by Lisa's sister, Dianne, they give the curious glimpses of what's going on in the kitchen, "which people really seem to get a kick out of, seeing the chefs in action, the hustle." Lisa says.

Their approach to their food, the embracing ambiance they create each night, their approachable menu—all of this is just more proof, as if we needed it, that one plus one can sometimes equal three, four, even five.

Chef Abby Harmon plating up Finnan Haddie with Soft-Boiled Eggs and Roasted Thyme Potatoes

Panna Cotta with Raspberry Sauce

Make ahead: first split the vanilla bean like a peapod, scrape out the seeds, and put seeds and bean halves into the cream overnight, covered and refrigerated.

For the panna cotta: In a 4-quart heavy-bottomed pot, heat the heavy cream with 1 cup sugar and vanilla. As the cream heats, prepare the gelatin (called "blooming") by soaking it 30-60 seconds in cold water until it is soft and pliable. Then, squeeze out the water from each leaf and drape it over the side of a large bowl. Boil the cream for 1 minute, then add the bloomed gelatin to the cream. Leaves will be sticky so work quickly. Stir and boil for 1½ minutes more. Whisk briefly and cool. Strain the cooked cream into the ramekins or other small bowls and chill.

For the raspberry sauce: cook 2 cups of the raspberries with 1 cup of sugar in a medium sauce pan until bubbly, about 5 minutes. Purée the fruit in a Cuisinart or blender and then strain through a sieve to eliminate seeds. Cook more if necessary until the sauce will coat the back of a spoon. When serving, unmold each panna cotta onto a small plate by running a knife dipped in hot water around the edge to loosen. Drizzle a little of the sauce around it, and top with fresh berries as desired. At Caiola's, we love raspberry sauce but change the fruit with the seasons.

Makes 10 individual servings

Ingredients:

- 2 quarts heavy cream (40% milkfat minimum)
- 2 cups granulated sugar
- 1 vanilla bean
- 5 leaves pastrymaker's gelatin
- 2+ cups raspberries, fresh or frozen

Panna Cotta with Raspberry Sauce

Above: Chef Lee Skawinski - Cinque Terre
Middle: Chef Steve Corry - 555

Below: Chef Sam Hayward and farmer Frank Gross - Fore Street

Above: Chef Rob Evans - Hugo's Restaurant
Below: Chef Chad Souders - Old Port Sea Grill

Cinque Terre

For Lee Skawinski, executive chef and part-owner, with Dan Kary, of Cinque Terre on Wharf Street, 2001 was a big year. With just the two of them at the helm after a re-organization, they began to make big changes, focusing in on a more purely authentic Italian/Ligurian cuisine driven by the bountiful produce of Kary's Grand View Farm in Greene.

Skawinski could shape more of the menu directly from what he and Kary chose to grow each season, his previous experience as a pasta maker found a niche in a pasta room in the restaurant's renovated cellar, and a new prep kitchen there also allowed his crew to more easily make their own sausages and *salumi* from whole animals in a clean space designed to their needs.

These days, when Chef Skawinski runs out of radicchio, he can, most months of the year, pick up the phone and put in an order to the farm. He won't have it for a day, but neither would he buy the commercial variety they sell in most groceries.

"It amazes me," he says, "how much like radicchio they can make those heads look, except that they taste almost like plain lettuce. That's not radicchio. Our seeds come from Italy, we grow them at the farm, and *that's* radicchio, with a nice bitterness and a complicated structure, not just one flavor. When we go to make a radicchio risotto, we'll crumble in some Hahn's End Bleu Velvet cheese, the rice will turn this incredible magenta, and the richness of the cheese will need that bit of bite from the radicchio."

At the farm, they grow only Italian varieties, whether it is squash, root vegetables, greens and lettuces, or the colorful broccolinis and cauliflowers and eggplants. "When you can source things that are so traditional variety-wise, like *delicata* and *marina di chiogga* squashes or Treviso radicchio," Skawinski says, "and real *puntarella* or incredible *quattro*," the first a kind of a dandelion, the second a variegated slightly bitter lettuce, "that just gives the food so much because you're cooking with exactly what you're supposed to be cooking with *and* we're growing it ourselves *and* in the way it should be grown to be the healthiest, freshest, just the best thing it can be. Of course, we can't grow everything, and I have relied a lot on Laughing Stock Farm and Farm Fresh Connection and lots of these smaller farms that are so good at raising what we don't—potatoes, tomatoes, carrots, whatever we need."

As for the cuisine, Skawinski calls what he does just plain country Italian cooking with a seacoast influence, the whole directly inspired by the real Cinque Terre, a coastal preserve in Liguria, on the Sea of Genoa. "We keep everybody happy while helping them to understand, this is what simplicity is about, smaller portions, lots of vegetables in the first plates then building up to richer, more complex dishes later, a bite or two of very good artisanal cheese at the end."

Take the Maine turkey and *delicata* squash ravioli with a walnut *parmigiano* sauce, an adaptation of a dish built around the ingredients you'd find in a typical

Chef Lee Skawinaki

Chef Skawinski at a Glance

Where do you find your inspiration?

In the traveling that I do, that month in Italy every year.

Do you have a spice or a flavor that pleases you?

Black pepper/fennel pollen/sea salt or capers/anchovies/garlic.

Is there a book that has influenced you lately?

The Food of a Younger Land by Mark Kurlansky.

When you're not cooking, what do you do to relax?

Travel, to New York five or six times a year, a month in Italy.

Do you have a favorite cheese?

Gorgonzola dolce.

Stuffed Roasted Rabbit Loin with Mushrooms & Prosciutto

For the stuffing: heat the olive oil in a medium sauté pan, add fennel, garlic, and shallot and cook until softened but not browned. Add the sage, wine, bread cubes, and toss to combine, then season to taste with salt and pepper. Refrigerate until cool.

To stuff the rabbit: on a large cutting board, lay one slice of prosciutto so that the long side is parallel to you. Lay more slices next to it with each overlapping the previous by ½" to make a rectangle about 1' long by 4-5" wide. (You will use fewer slices if they are both long and wide.) Take one piece of rabbit and lay it on the left side of the prosciutto so that the thinner belly edge is aligned with the longer edge closest to you and the thicker loin is in the middle. Lay the second loin beside it to the right. Don't worry if loin does not cover prosciutto perfectly. Put the stuffing in a mounded line left to right down the middle of the square of rabbit. Starting at the edge closest to you, roll prosciutto/rabbit towards the back of the cutting board to make a prosciutto-wrapped tube. Place on a rack on a sheet pan and chill for 30 minutes.

To serve: preheat oven to 375°F. Roast on rack over sheet pan for 30 minutes. Remove from pan and let rest. Deglaze sheet pan with chicken stock and butter and reserve resulting liquid in small pan. While rabbit rests, sauté sliced mushrooms in the butter. To plate, slice loin into medallions about ¾" wide, arrange 3 slices in the center of each plate, spoon deglazing sauce over them then garnish with sautéed mushrooms and fennel fronds.

Serves 4 as an entrée

Ingredients

Rabbit and Mushroom Garnish
- 2 rabbit loins with belly flaps
- 2 tablespoons chicken stock
- 1 tablespoon butter
- 1 cup seasonal wild mushrooms, washed and sliced
- 2 tablespoons butter
- 1 teaspoon fresh thyme leaves, chopped
- 2 tablespoons fennel fronds, in 1" lengths

Stuffing
- 4-6 slices prosciutto
- 2 tablespoons olive oil
- 1 cup mushrooms, sliced
- 2 tablespoons fennel, in ½" dice
- 1 clove garlic, peeled and finely chopped
- 1 small shallot, peeled and finely chopped
- 3 sage leaves
- 1 cup freshly toasted small bread cubes
- 2 tablespoons white wine
- Salt and black pepper

Stuffed Roasted Rabbit Loin with Mushrooms & Prosciutto

Chef Lee Skawinski preparing Stuffed Roasted Rabbit Loin with Mushrooms & Prosciutto

Lamb Loin with Roasted Tomato and Salsa Verde

For the tomatoes: preheat oven to 400°F. Halve the tomatoes lengthwise, put them in a small bowl and toss with two pinches of salt. Let rest half-hour then drain, put cut side up on sheet pan and season with salt, pepper, rosemary, and parsley. Lower oven temp to 250°F. and roast tomatoes until nicely brown, 3-4 hours, then top with cheese and drizzle with olive oil

For the salsa verde: purée all the ingredients in the bowl of a food processor and season with salt and pepper.

For the lamb and marinade: trim the excess fat off the loin and cut into 12 equal size rounds. Mix all marinade ingredients in a bowl, then put the lamb slices into a 1-gallon Ziploc bag and pour the marinade over them. Let stand, refrigerated, at least 3 hours.

To serve: preheat oven grill for 15 minutes or let outdoor charcoal or gas grill reach maximum heat. Grill the loin slices medium rare, about 4 minutes total, flipping once after 2 minutes, then set aside to rest. Season with salt and pepper and drizzle with olive oil. At Cinque Terre, we serve this on rectangular dishes and plated restaurant-style, as shown. For a more informal plating, overlap lamb slices slightly, 3 to a plate, spoon salsa verde over the top and put two roasted tomato halves to one side. A favorite side dish is raw white turnip, shredded and in a shallot vinaigrette with olive oil, Trebbiano vinegar, salt and pepper, and a little honey.

Serves 4

Ingredients

Tomatoes

8 small vine-ripened tomatoes
1 teaspoon fresh rosemary, chopped
1 teaspoon fresh parsley, chopped
Olive oil for drizzling
3 tablespoons grated Pecorino
3 tablespoons bread crumbs
Salt and black pepper

Salsa Verde

2 tablespoons savory leaves
10 sage leaves
1 bunch parsley, rinsed and de-stemmed
2 walnuts
1 tablespoon capers
1 tablespoon anchovies
1 clove garlic
3 ounces extra virgin olive oil
1 tablespoon bread crumbs
1 tablespoon Trebbiano or white wine
   vinegar

Lamb and Marinade

1½ pounds lamb loin
2 tablespoons extra virgin olive oil
1 tablespoon walnut oil
3 sage leaves
1 shallot, peeled and chopped

Left: Lamb Loin with Roasted Tomato and Salsa Verde

> *Maybe we went to Venice and ate in six different places in one day, just little snacks, but we'll talk about every one. What did you think about thos sardines, that speck, the fennel pollen in that sauce? Everyone contribute. and I get it all down on paper. When we come back, I give the guys all the ideas that we came across, and we get to work. It keeps it fresh.* "

Ligurian backyard. "There," Skawinski says, "it's called *pan-sotti* ravioli, every recipe with a little different green or squash. Here, we make a great little fall combination. Touch of sweet with the squash, richness with the slow-roasted turkey, a straight-up little local dish complemented with a local ingredient, walnuts, in a sauce that's just a little pasta water and some cheese, and the crushed nuts. This is simplicity."

Though Skawinski's previous career, spent in high-end hotel restaurant kitchens and destination restaurants from Santa Barbara to Boston, gave him a front-row seat for the food revolution that swept from coast to coast beginning in the late '80s, it wasn't until he moved to Maine ten years ago and found Cinque Terre and the Kary farm that he found his real groove.

Everything since has been refining—and bringing his team of sous chefs along with him. That includes taking them as a group to one region of Italy for a few weeks each year, there to spend each day exploring, learning, but also eating everywhere from street stalls to fish shacks to humble *enotecas* and *osterias*. "Every third day," Skawinski says, "we'll sit down in the morning and review what we've eaten. Maybe we went to Venice and ate in six different places in one day, just little snacks, but we'll talk about every one. What did you think about those sardines, that speck, the fennel pollen in that sauce? Everyone contributes, and I get it all down on paper. When we come back, I give the guys all the ideas that we came across, and we get to work. It keeps it fresh."

Above: On the line at Cinque Terre

Stuffed Poussins with Apple Mostarda

For the mostarda: preheat oven to 400°F. Put the apples on a sheet pan and roast until caramelized and dried about 20-25 minutes. Put the wine, sugar, mustard seed, and mustard powder into a small saucepan and bring to a boil, then reduce to simmer. Add roasted apples and combine all ingredients, seasoning with salt and pepper. Set aside. Can be made a day ahead and refrigerated.

For the stuffing: heat 1 tablespoon of the olive oil in a medium sauté pan, add the livers and hearts, carrot, onion, carrot, garlic, thyme. Cook for 2-3 minutes tossing once or twice to mix, until onion is soft. Add brandy and then scrape up browned bits from bottom of pan as the alcohol evaporates. Season with salt and pepper, then chill until needed.

For the poultry: preheat oven to 400°F. Debone breasts and legs, or ask your butcher to, so you end up with 4 portions, each of which is 1 leg and 1 breast with the wing attached. Put one tablespoon of stuffing into the cavity of each leg where the bone was, then wrap the leg in one slice of speck. In a sauté pan large enough to fit all the pieces, heat 2 tablespoons of olive oil with 2 tablespoons butter. Over medium heat, cook breasts and legs skin side down until crispy brown, about 3-4 minutes, and starting with legs, which may take longer. Turn legs to sear all sides, flip breasts, and finish cooking 2-3 more minutes. Place all pieces into the hot oven and roast 5 minutes, remove and let rest.

To serve: add the apple mostarda to the poultry cooking pan and mix with pan juices. For each plate, slice the leg into two rounds and put them off-center, lean the breast against the slices. Spoon on the mostarda sauce. At Cinque Terre, we serve this with a simple butter-seared potato cake and roasted Brussels sprouts, but a simple risotto or other rice side would work well, too.

Serves 4

Ingredients

2 1-1½ pound poussins or game hens
4 slices speck ham

Apple Mostarda

4 apples, peeled, cored, and diced in ½"
   dice
2 ounces dry white wine
2 ounces sugar
1 teaspoon mustard powder
1 teaspoon yellow mustard seed
Salt and black pepper

Stuffing

Livers and hearts from birds, chopped
   fine
½ small carrot, finely diced
½ small yellow onion, finely diced
½ rib celery, finely diced
1 small clove garlic, peeled and sliced
¼ cup good bread, in ¼" dice
1 ounce brandy
2 tablespoons unsalted butter
3 tablespoons extra virgin olive oil
Salt and pepper

Stuffed Poussins with Apple Mostarda

five fifty five

When Steve Corry and his wife, Michelle, bought 555 Congress Street in 2003 with the intention of turning it into their unique version of a white tablecloth restaurant, they heard plenty of doubters. Today, after an expansion offering a separate, intimate, bar and lounge space, an evolved menu, and an almost overnight

discovery by the national press, the "Nays" have turned not just into "Yeas" but "You bet – and can I have the mussels with roasted garlic and pickled peppers with that?"

Take a few steps into the restaurant's soothing and restrained brick and copper interior, warm tile floors at your feet and a central mezzanine soaring above, and check your assumptions at the door. Yes, the Corrys certainly deliver everything you expect – faultless wine and table service and a lush array of menu choices tuned to the seasons and the bounty of Maine's farms and seacoast. But the pair, Steve in the kitchen and Michelle on the floor, aren't shy about springing the best kind of surprises on the diner. Are those chunks of lobster and black truffle in your mac 'n cheese? Yes, and that would be four ounces of lobster and generous shavings of truffle because, as Steve says, "The nature of a chef is to be hospitable, welcoming—and generous. If you don't feel that way, you should probably look for other work."

Chef Steve Corry

While Steve is pleasing your belly, Michelle ups the ante in the service department, coddling her customers in the nicest of ways. They go so far, she says, "as to call certain customers when special dishes and wines come back on the menu, reserve particular seats, order in this bottle or that. We have a customer who loves our pastry chef's 'peppermint patties'. They are not always on the menu, but we make sure we have some when she comes. Her name is Pat, and last time she came in the chef embossed the letter 'P' on them for her!"

They even understand that, sometimes, people want permission to eat with their hands. Take the experience of those mussels, a full pound of Bangs Island mussels steamed in white wine and garnished with lemon/chive butter, roasted garlic, and spicy house-pickled peppers. Your server delivers it in a cast iron pot, "with lots of homemade bread because you'll want to soak up that broth and you need to get your fingers in there to eat the mussels," as Steve points out. "But after, we bring steamed hot towels and finger bowls with lemon water so you can clean up before the next course."

The two certainly have earned their restaurant chops. In Napa, he cooked at Domaine Chandon while she worked across the street at the French Laundry. Later and locally, she found a niche at the White Barn Inn and he at its sister restaurant, Grissini's. All of this experience they bring to every plate, every table at **five fifty five**. "We worked unbelievably hard, so many hours!" Steve points out. "And we paid attention the whole time. When we weren't working, we were eating at others' restaurants, always asking, what's good, why, how can we do something like this?"

Chef Corry at a Glance

Where do you find your inspiration?

My love for eating different things, everywhere.

Do you have a spice or a flavor that pleases you?

I love heat, black pepper, chorizo, pickled cherry peppers.

Do you have any chef heroes?

Robert Curry, of L'Auberge du Soleil in Napa, who mentored me.

Favorite midnight snack?

Midnight for us is actually dinnertime.

Is there a book that has influenced you recently?

Cormac McCarthy's *The Road*.

Do you have a kitchen utensil that is particularly pleasing to you?

I don't have any knife or tool fetishes. If it's sharp and it works . . .

Bangs Island Mussels with Roasted Garlic and Pickled Peppers

For the pickled peppers and roasted garlic: preheat oven to 300°F. Halve each bulb of garlic horizontally, and douse with 1 tablespoon of the olive oil. Roast in a small pan in the oven about 1-1½ hours until garlic is golden and quite soft. Cool. When cool, squeeze each clove into the bowl of a mortar and pestle and crush into a paste. Reserve. Put 2 tablespoons of olive oil into a heavy-bottomed 3-quart sauce pan and heat over medium, add carrot, celery, and onion, and cook until onion is translucent but not browned, about 5 minutes. Add water and vinegar and bring to a boil. Add salt. Return to a boil. Remove liquid from heat. Wash the peppers and put them in the bottom of a glass or ceramic lidded container of at least 3-quart capacity. Cover peppers with hot liquid. Cool, then refrigerate and allow to pickle for 2-3 weeks.

For the mussels: heat very large high-sided sauté pan over high heat until it is very hot. Add a splash of oil, then the pickled peppers, bell peppers, and roasted garlic, and sauté quickly, about 30 seconds. Add mussels and toss. Add white wine and reduce liquid by half, then add butter, chives, lemon juice, and salt. Toss and then cover mussels with a lid and allow them to steam open. Discard any that do not open. Remove open mussels from the pan with slotted spoon, leaving sauce. Let sauce reduce over medium heat until thickened and then pour over the mussels. Serve with crusty grilled bread. At 555, we use local providers—Snell Farm garlic, Freedom Farm peppers, and Bangs Island mussels, and we encourage you to use your own local, organic ingredients.

Serves 4 as a hearty appetizer

Ingredients

Pickled Pepper and Roasted Garlic Garnishes

1 quart water
1 quart white vinegar
½ cup kosher salt
1 pound hot cherry peppers
1 carrot, in ½" dice
1 celery stalk, in ½" dice
1 yellow onion, in ½" dice
2 bulbs whole garlic
3 tablespoons olive oil

Mussels

4 tablespoons orange bell pepper, in ¼" dice
3 tablespoons pickled cherry peppers, seeded and minced fine
4 tablespoons roasted garlic
2 pounds Bangs Island mussels
1 tablespoon canola oil
1½ cups dry white wine
6 ounces local butter
2 tablespoons chopped chives
Lemon juice to taste
Salt to taste

Bangs Island Mussels with Roasted Garlic and Pickled Peppers

Truffled Lobster Mac 'n Cheese

Honey–Pear Soufflé

Preheat oven to 375°F. Prepare 4 6-ounce ramekins: melt 3 tablespoons of the butter. Using a pastry brush, grease bottom and insides of ramekins thoroughly, then pour a couple of tablespoons of sugar in each. Shake ramekin around, coating the bottom and sides completely. Pour out excess sugar. Clean the top rim and outsides of the ramekin with a damp cloth.

Make the pastry cream: combine the honey, pear purée, heavy cream, spices, and salt in a small sauce pan. Heat on low, stirring often until well combined and just simmering. Meanwhile, combine the 6 yolks, flour, and 6 tablespoons of the sugar in a bowl. Gradually add honey mixture to yolk mixture, whisking until incorporated. Place mixture in a saucepan and cook on low heat, stirring constantly until slightly thickened, about 5 minutes. Remove from heat and add the remaining tablespoon of butter. Pour mixture in a large bowl and cool to room temperature.

Make the meringue: in a stand mixer, whip the 6 egg whites and the cream of tartar until foamy. Continue to beat on medium high, while gradually adding the remaining 6 tablespoons of sugar. Whip until whites will hold stiff peaks.

Very gently fold a third of the meringue into the pastry cream. Repeat two more times until all the meringue is incorporated, making sure not to deflate the whites. Spoon enough of the mixture into two ramekins so that the mixture comes above the tops. Holding the ramekin over the bowl containing the rest of the mixture, use the flat side of a knife blade to scrape excess back into the bowl. Repeat with remaining ramekins. Clean the outside and top of the ramekins quickly with a damp cloth. Place the soufflés on a sheet tray and place in the oven for 12 minutes. Serve immediately.

Serves 4

Ingredients
½ cup honey
¾ cup Perfect Purée brand pear purée
¼ cup flour
½ teaspoon salt
¼ cup heavy cream
¼ cup butter (2 oz.)
¾ teaspoon cinnamon
¾ cup sugar, plus more for ramekins
½ teaspoon ground ginger
6 eggs, separated
Pinch of nutmeg
½ teaspoon cream of tartar

Honey–Pear Soufflé

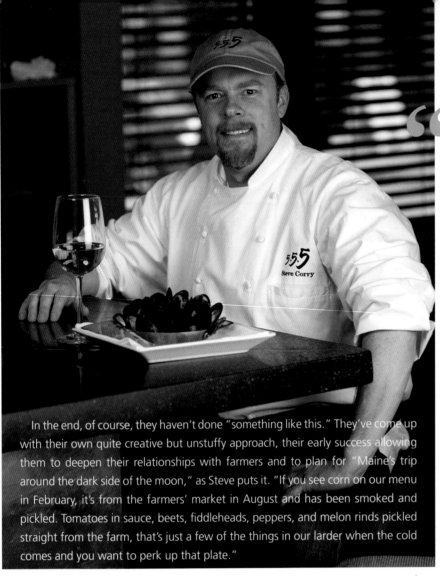

In the end, of course, they haven't done "something like this." They've come up with their own quite creative but unstuffy approach, their early success allowing them to deepen their relationships with farmers and to plan for "Maine's trip around the dark side of the moon," as Steve puts it. "If you see corn on our menu in February, it's from the farmers' market in August and has been smoked and pickled. Tomatoes in sauce, beets, fiddleheads, peppers, and melon rinds pickled straight from the farm, that's just a few of the things in our larder when the cold comes and you want to perk up that plate."

While you can always get simpler dishes like a burger or steak or great cut of chicken or fish on the bar and lounge menu, in the dining room the menu tends to more substantial, artful cuisine. His creativity begins in sometimes whimsical presentations that do everything to relax and amuse the diner, like that "lobster mac 'n cheese", or an item called "3 Little Pigs", say, where a fat, perfectly roasted chop shares a plate with house baked beans larded with pork belly, a flag made of bacon flying over the whole. Whimsical, yes, but lush, too, with what Steve calls "sometimes outside of the box food pairings. Sure, we'll do snails with garlic and parsley and butter, traditional and fancy. But," here he smiles wickedly, "my favorite is more, let's go green garlic, chorizo butter, and pickled mushrooms with the snails. You might think it's the same until you dig in, then wow! So, it's a little more crazy, more fun, and just as delicious."

Whether you swing tried or true or choose to explore more adventurous plates, Steve and Michelle work very hard to make you happy, and in every way. "We love," Michelle says, "that people comment on the entire experience and not just the food. They even ask me who are decorator is, when it was just Steve and I. Most important is that people leave thinking it was special, an occasion and not just a meal."

Pepper Crusted Divers Scallops with Carrot Vanilla Emulsion

For the emulsion: peel and juice carrot. Warm juice over low heat in small stainless steel pot. Split the vanilla bean in half lengthwise and scrape the seeds out with a knife, adding both beans and seeds to the juice. Slowly whisk the cold butter into the warm carrot juice. Add the lemon juice, and season with salt. Set pot in larger pan half filled with warm tap water until serving.

For the purée: core, clean, and chop the fennel bulbs into 1" dice, then sauté in the butter over medium heat for 5 minutes. Add Sambuca and flambé. Cover with cream. Braise over low heat, covered, for about 30 minutes until tender. Purée in food processor or pass through fine sieve. Peel and quarter the potatoes and simmer them in salted water until tender. Strain and run through food mill or ricer. Begin adding potato to fennel until you acheive a purée the consistency of velvety mashed potatoes. Season to taste with salt.

For the scallops: salt the scallops. Spread the black pepper in a thin layer over a large plate, and coat one flat side of each scallop with pepper. Heat two 12" sauté pans over very high heat. Add 2 tablespoons of vegetable oil to each pan. Place 8 scallops pepper side down in each pan when oil is very hot, and sear until golden brown. Turn heat down to medium. Add half the cold, cubed butter to each pan, then turn over scallops and finish, about 2 minutes. Put a small mound of fennel purée in center of four shallow bowls or plates. Pour a shallow pool of sauce around the purée. Place 4 scallops, evenly spaced, in a circle around purée in each bowl, resting part of scallop on the purée. At the restaurant, we use a simple and very bright accompaniment like baby carrots, pearl onions, and fresh soy beans, arranging them between the scallops on each plate and adding a scallion garnish.

Serves 4 as an entrée

Ingredients

Carrot Vanilla Emulsion
1 large organic carrot
4 ounces unsalted butter in cubes
1 teaspoon lemon juice
Salt to taste
1 vanilla bean

Fennel and Yukon Gold Potato Purée
2 fennel bulbs
2 large Yukon gold potatoes
1 large russet potato
1 cup cream
4 ounces butter
½ cup Sambuca or other anisette
Salt to taste

Scallops
16 large Maine divers scallops (8-10count/lb)
½ cup freshly ground black peppercorns
4 tablespoons vegetable oil
2 ounces cold butter, cubed
Salt

Pepper Crusted Divers Scallops with Carrot Vanilla Emulsion

Fore Street Restaurant

When you enter Fore Street Restaurant a block from Portland's waterfront, you could be forgiven for thinking that you'd taken the wrong door and walked into a working kitchen in full swing instead. The eye is drawn first to a 40-foot-long, red brick hotline dominating one wall, the red-tinged mouth of a wood-fired oven at one

end and at the other a massive turnspit, ten feet of grill shimmering with the heat of its glowing coals in between. Tiers of tables rise to walls of windows looking out over Portland Harbor, warm wooden floors echo your steps underfoot, and the air is heavy with the agreeable smells of applewood smoke and grilling meat. After 5 o'clock, the line crackles with the energy of a half-dozen scurrying sous-chefs slinging pans, calling orders to as many waitresses, and a garde-manger opening oysters and running greens and vegetables from the glass-walled pantry just off the entrance.

If you thought this was some trendy imitator bringing the diners into the kitchen, well, Sam Hayward, Fore Street's co-owner and a chef with more than 30 years of cooking behind him, conceived this restaurant about ten years ahead of the curve, innovating as he has done in so many things.

Chef Sam Hayward

Hayward is Maine's answer to Alice Waters but cast in a distinctly New England mold, keenly tuned to a sensibility where no fish is wasted, all cuts of meat are treated like prime, and no root vegetable goes unexploited. While this comes partly from a natural frugality and horror of wasting food, it is also tied deeply to his origins as a chef, a few summers spent as staff cook for the scientists and students at Shoals Marine Lab on Appledore Island isolated in the Gulf of Maine. There, working with "deeply acculturated Yankees," as he recalls, "the respect for raw materials, their most efficient and best use, this was beaten into me until it took on a moral dimension, that it is a moral obligation to use food wisely and responsibly, to keep our local food culture and our regional food culture alive and to preserve the food resources that New England has always cherished."

In practice this means he has been working hand-in-hand with local organic farmers, animal growers, and fishermen, some of them, since the early '80s and can tell you, often, not only whose boat your halibut came in on and when, but

Hayward is Maine's answer to Alice Waters but cast in a distinctly New England mold . . .

Chef Hayward at a Glance

Is there a spice mixture or special flavor you like to sneak into a dish?

I like fresh herbs out of the garden, particularly some of the weirdos – lovage, winter savory, lavender.

Is there a country whose cuisine you think underrated?

Where did authentic Cuban cooking migrate to?

Do you have a favorite kitchen implement?

I love my terracotta cooking pots called *cazuelas*—I have them in all sizes and shapes.

Favorite midnight snack?

Something simple, an omelette maybe.

What was a recent book that inspired you?

The Whole Beast: Nose to Tail Eating by Fergus Henderson

Pork Belly With Carola Potatoes And Sauerkraut

For the pork: rub pork belly with sea salt and black pepper and place in a ceramic or glass container over the bay leaves, thyme, and rosemary. Cover and refrigerate overnight. The second day, preheat the oven to 450°F. Choose a non-reacting roasting pan just larger than the pork belly. Layer the sliced carrot, celery, leeks, the garlic cloves, and the ginger-root slices in the bottom of the roasting pan, and place the pork belly over the vegetables. Roast the pork belly for 20 to 30 minutes, or until the surface is well browned. Add the beer and enough chicken stock to come halfway up the thickness of the pork belly. Cover closely with foil. Reduce the oven temperature to 250°F.

Braise the pork belly until fork-tender, 6 to 8 hours, replenishing the braising liquid to original level when necessary. When done, cool the pork to room temperature in its braising liquid. Remove the meat to another pan and strain the braising liquid through a fine sieve, discarding the solids. Chill the liquid and lift off the hardened fat that rises to its surface, saving it.

For the potatoes and sauerkraut: place the potatoes and garlic cloves in a saucepan. Cover with cool water, and heat over high flame until simmering. Adjust the flame to keep the water at a bare simmer, about 180°F. Do not boil. Simmer until the potatoes are almost tender when pierced with a skewer or thin knife blade, about thirty minutes. Drain the potatoes and cover with cool water to arrest the cooking. When cool enough to handle, peel off the skins. Drain the sauerkraut in a sieve, pressing on the solids to squeeze out most of the moisture.

Final assembly: preheat the oven to 375°F. Melt 3-4 tablespoons of the reserved pork fat in a heavy non-reacting gratin dish. Add the peeled potatoes, toss to coat with the fat, and move to one side. Add the drained sauerkraut to the gratin dish beside the potatoes and sprinkle on black pepper to taste, the chopped thyme and rosemary, and season the potatoes with sea salt. Place the pork belly on the sauerkraut, and pour over it one cup of the reserved braising liquid. Heat thoroughly in the preheated oven, at least twenty minutes. To serve, slice the pork belly into half-inch slices, and lay the slices over the sauerkraut.

Serves 6-8

Ingredients

Pork Belly

3 pounds fresh pork belly in one piece, skin removed
1½ tablespoons Maine sea salt
2 teaspoons fresh-milled black pepper
3 bay leaves, crumbled
3-4 sprigs fresh thyme
2 sprigs fresh rosemary
1 medium carrot, peeled, sliced into ½" thick rounds
2 ribs celery cut into ½ inch dice
1 medium leek, white part with a little green, sliced diagonally - ½" pieces
3 garlic cloves, peeled, crushed
1" piece of fresh ginger-root, peeled, sliced thin
24 ounces Allagash White or other Belgian-style wheat beer
1 to 2 quarts chicken stock

Potatoes

2 pounds Carola potatoes or other yellow-fleshed fingerlings
4 cloves garlic, peeled, whole

Sauerkraut

1 pound Morse's sauerkraut
Reserved braising liquid & chilled pork fat
Sea salt and black pepper to taste
2 teaspoons chopped fresh thyme leaves
½ teaspoon chopped fresh rosemary leaves

Pork Belly With Carola Potatoes And Sauerkraut

Braised Lamb Shoulder

Roasted Maine Lobster With Wild Mushrooms

For the mushrooms: clean and trim the mushrooms. Slice them into thick sections. Melt about 3 tablespoons of the butter over high flame in a non-reacting skillet. Add the mushrooms, season with sea salt and pepper to taste, and sauté quickly just until tender. Using a slotted spoon, set them aside in a bowl. With the skillet back on the flame, add shallots, toss quickly without browning, and, off the flame, pour in all the cider. On simmer, reduce the cider to half its volume, lower flame, and swirl in butter in pieces, using a wire whisk to achieve a creamy sauce. Off the heat, season with sea salt and black pepper. Add the reserved mushrooms to the skillet, and toss to combine. Keep the mushroom mixture warm as you prepare the lobsters.

For the lobsters: preheat the oven to 450°F. Bring a large pot of heavily salted water to a rolling boil and fill a sink with half water, half ice. Remove the rubber bands from the lobsters' claws. Drop the lobsters into the boiling water, replace the lid, and poach the lobsters about 4 minutes, then drop them immediately into the sink to stop the cooking. The shells should be mottled red, but the lobsters will be undercooked.

After lobsters are chilled, remove them from the water. Twist off the claws. Separate the arm-like knuckles from the claws. With stout shears, cut open the knuckles, crack the claws and remove the meat. Twist the tails from the bodies. With a heavy, sharp knife, split the bodies lengthwise. Split the tails lengthwise, and remove the black, tube-like, intestinal tract. Arrange the lobster tails, shells down, in a heavy roasting pan just large enough to contain all the lobster pieces in a single layer. Add the lobster body pieces, shells down, and divide the knuckle and claw meat among the body halves. Season all the meat with sea salt and a turn of the peppermill. Divide the sautéed mushroom mixture among the lobster pieces, spooning the butter sauce over them equally. Mix the chopped parsley, chervil, tarragon, thyme, and chives together and scatter them evenly over the lobsters.

Roast the lobsters in the preheated oven about 10 minutes, agitating the pan once or twice, until the shells have turned deeper red, and the lobster meat has firmed. Serve half or full lobster portions on individual plates, spooning over them any liquids that remain in the bottom of the roasting pan.

Serves 4

Ingredients

12 tablespoons unsalted butter, chilled, cut into ½" pieces
1¼ pound fresh wild mushrooms—chanterelles, hen-of-the-woods, or porcini—or cultivated mushrooms like shiitake and oyster
2 medium shallots, peeled, minced fine
1 cup dry hard cider or dry white wine
Maine sea salt and fresh milled black pepper to taste
1 tablespoon chopped fresh parsley
1 tablespoon chopped fresh chervil leaves
1 teaspoon chopped fresh thyme leaves
½ teaspoon chopped fresh tarragon leaves
1 tablespoon snipped fresh chives
4 live 1½ pound Maine lobsters

Roasted Maine Lobster With Wild Mushrooms

where the cardoons garnishing it were grown and where the farmer's daughter went to college. He is a founding member of the Maine Organic Farmers and Gardeners Association, and the list of contributing providers on his menu reads like a roll call of the best and brightest—and most stalwart—on the vibrant Maine local and sustainable food scene.

Throughout this long career, Sam reflects that his cooking hasn't so much evolved as devolved. "There was a period in my life," he says, "where I arranged things on the plates in a careful way and strained my sauces 15 times. About fifteen years ago, I began paring down, moving to incredibly simple preparations and presentations which to me were no less beautiful, but much more about the food itself than about the ideas I imposed on food. This is how I want to think of myself and Fore Street—as being part of a pure continuum that includes the raw production on the farm and the consumer at either end with me in the middle, performing some kind of distillation but bringing those two ends around into a circle."

Above: Lobster Chowder

In practice, this embracing philosophy means buying whole animals and fish and then applying timeworn New England cooking techniques such as braising, smoking, brining and curing to use every part to its fullest. The use of fire plays an elemental role, too, adding flavor as well as atmosphere. This approach also means barrels of homemade cider and wine vinegar maturing in the restaurant's basement, daily deliveries of foraged greens and wild mushrooms in season, shelves of house-made herb vinegars, infused oils, and salt lemons. It means a recent foray into house-cured charcuterie and salumi and experiments in dry-aging to take full advantage of Maine-raised all-natural pork and beef not available even five years ago.

"The restaurant is always collaborative," he says, "and now we can do nose-to-tail cooking and really put every part of the animal to best use. You know," he finishes, laughing, "now we have so many cooks trained in charcuterie that they compete to get their hands on organ meats and secondary cuts to use in their experiments, a lot of which do end up on the menu."

Goat Cheesecake With Fresh Cranberry Sauce

For the cheesecake: preheat the oven to 350°F. Generously butter the insides of six 6 ounce baking rings. Butter the bottom of a baking sheet pan large enough to contain all the rings without crowding. Add the sugar to the bowl of a blender. Process the sugar to reduce the grains almost to a powder. In the bowl of an electric mixer, combine the cream cheese, the goat cheese, vanilla bean essence, ground sugar, and flour. On low speed, mix these ingredients, scraping down the sides and beater frequently, until all of the sugar is incorporated, about 8 to 10 minutes.

Add the whole eggs and egg yolk. Continue to mix on low speed until smooth, scraping down the bowl once or twice. Place the baking rings on the baking pan. Spoon equal amounts of the cheese mixture into the rings. Tap the pan on a counter to settle the filling. Place the pan in the preheated oven. Bake 5 minutes, then reduce the heat to 300°F and continue baking an additional 12 to 15 minutes, or until filling seems firm when touched lightly. Don't overcook. Cool to room temperature.

For the fresh cranberry sauce: in a non-reacting saucepan, bring the raw sugar, cider, and lemon zest to a boil. Add half of the cranberries and bring back to a simmer. Simmer over low heat until all the berries have opened and spilled their liquefied contents. Pour the mixture into a wire sieve set over a bowl and allow the syrup to drain thoroughly, pressing solids with the back of a spoon or ladle. Return the syrup to the saucepan, and return to a boil over a high flame. Add the remaining cranberries, stir quickly, and reduce flame to a simmer. Watch carefully from this point. Gently fold the syrup over and through the berries just until the berries have softened, 3 or 4 minutes. Remove them from the heat and cool slightly.

To serve: lift the cheescakes in their rings from the baking pan with a spatula. Place them on serving plates, run a thin knife around the interior of each ring to loosen the filling, and lift off the ring. Spoon a little of the warm cranberry mixture over each cheesecake, and a little more on the plate.

6 Individual Portions

Ingredients

Cheesecake

¼ cup turbinado or other raw sugar
½ pound cream cheese, at room temperature
½ pound soft fresh goat cheese, (chèvre) minimally salted, at room temperature
1 vanilla bean, split, and the essence scraped from the insides
1 tablespoon all-purpose flour
2 eggs
1 egg yolk
2–3 tablespoons unsalted butter, for greasing the baking rings and baking pan

Cranberry Sauce

1¼ cup raw sugar
¼ cup sweet cider
Grated zest of ½ lemon
1 pound fresh Maine organic cranberries, washed and picked over, divided

Left: Goat Cheesecake With Fresh Cranberry Sauce

Hugo's Restaurant

Too cold, too far, too dull, too limited – these are the stereotypes all good Maine chefs have to overcome. And overcome them they have, in often ingenious ways. "In Maine, chefs, fisherman, farmers, and producers," says Hugo's chef/owner Rob Evans, "have had to work symbiotically, and together we have created a culinary scene like no other in the country. Most of us are small, we're flexible, and we roll with the times."

Chef Evans, and his wife, Nancy Pugh Evans, have chosen a course that draws its inspiration from traditional New England dishes and ways of cooking, but then reinterprets, deconstructs, and reinvents them to arrive at a place perhaps more experimental than many of its Portland neighbors on Restaurant Row. While he serves himself a portion of the liberation and the theatricality of molecular gastronomy, this is balanced by many influences and isn't limited to the in-your-face. "All that means," he says, "is that we've replaced the pretentious side of that style with fun. And, yes, at the end of the day you still have to feed people real food."

Fun means a very casual atmosphere, small plates to full tasting menus, and a genial waitstaff who explains the food and wine in down-to-earth language.

Fun means that Rob makes his own funky bar snacks like homemade fritos and cheese puffs (with parmesan and truffle), offers pig's ear cracklings and pirogies filled with foie gras. The dinner menu is a good example of his approach of pairing something more daring with something familiar and reassuring. "We make a lobster sashimi – with Butte fries." Rob says. These are organic Maine potatoes cut long and thin, poached in oil, fried, then seasoned with caper and herb powder. They come in a tall metal stand inside a cone of Kraft paper, a small pot of truffle ketchup perched on one side. "Ketchup and fries, yeah, but then paired with a beef tartare, a lobster sashimi, it encourages people to try new things. We make mini green apple popsicles as a palate cleanser. Who doesn't like popsicles? I do a smoked milkshake with Maine maple syrup." Which doesn't mean you can't get a beautiful piece of Maine halibut or maybe braised pork belly or rabbit, depending on the season.

Just steps down the street, you'll find Duckfat, his alter ego eatery which opens early and is a place where he has distilled his love for just a handful of items—duck, potatoes, fresh-baked bread, and mayo—into a decadent mini-menu. Just a few pananis – variations on the deli theme with a twist like duck confit or corned beef tongue or house meatloaf, join a fistful of salads and those Belgian frites, handcut organic Maine potatoes fried in duckfat to crisp perfection and served with funky mayos. Homemade soda pops and powdered sugar beignets fill out the menu in a place that put the fat in funky and where thirty-something Portlanders can be found tucking in at all hours.

And that's Rob Evans, too, a deceptively simple package in which you'll find all kinds of surprises for every sense, where the dinner is the show, and the chef magician, entertainer, and alchemist all rolled into one.

Chef Rob Evans

Chef Evans at a Glance

Where do you find inspiration?

In everyday things — eating anything anywhere, a book or magazine, a bag of Fritos.

Do you have any chef heroes?

Keller is one, Grant Achatz, of course. Patrick O'Connell and Daniel Boulud.

When you're not cooking, what do you do to relax?

Ride my BMW GS1100, going off-road to explore, motorcycle camping.

Is there a spice mixture you favor?

Cinnamon, star anise, allspice, through the winter mostly, for almost anything.

What's your favorite midnight snack?

Ben & Jerry's Coffee Heath Bar ice cream.

What's your favorite cheese?

Cloth-aged 3-year cheddar from Shelburne Farms in Vermont.

Pan-Seared Maine Cod with Potato Broth & Oyster Crackers

For the crackers: preheat oven to 425°F. Warm the milk 1 minute in microwave and stir in yeast until dissolved. In the bowl of a mixer, combine salt and flour, then milk/yeast mixture using paddle attachment. Switch to dough hook attachment and knead 2 minutes. Divide into 4 balls, cover with damp towel, rest 1 hour. With pasta roller attachment or pasta machine on first setting, roll each ball into a sheet, let rest 1 minute, repeat 4 or 5 times. Cut the cracker shapes from the sheets with a fluted, circular dough cutter about 1" in diameter. Let raw crackers rest uncovered 10 minutes. Bake 3 minutes in hot oven, rotate pan front to back, back 3 more minutes. Remove from oven and cool 20 minutes, reduce oven temperature to 250°F. and bake again until dry and crispy, 35-45 minutes, checking frequently after ½ an hour. Cool on rack.

For the potato broth: to a 2-quart pan add leeks, bacon fat, garlic, shallots, bay leaf, white wine, vinegar and crushed red pepper. Simmer on low until almost dry. Add 4 cups of clam broth and turn heat up to a boil. Simmer for ½ hour and strain. Grate raw potato with a cheese grater into the broth. Add thyme sprigs and simmer for 20 minutes. Strain potato broth and return to a clean pan. Add crème fraiche and salt & pepper to taste. Set aside in pan to warm later.

For the cod loin: heat skillet on high, add canola oil, and season cod pieces with salt and pepper. Turn heat down to medium and cook until crispy golden brown. Flip pieces and cook for 1 minute before removing from heat. Spoon 4 ounces of warmed potato broth into 4 bowls. Drizzle with olive oil and sprinkle with the thyme leaves. Place 1 piece of cod in broth, garnish with a few crackers and serve immediately. At Hugo's we sometimes serve this with 4 ounces of picked, steamed periwinkles added to each bowl before the cod as well as a crispy cod skin garnish.

Serves 8 as light entrée

Ingredients

Crackers
¾ ounce Dry Active Yeast
¾ cup whole milk
1 teaspoon salt
1½ cup flour

Potato Broth
1 teaspoon bacon fat
1 leek, cut into ½" dice
1 clove garlic, peeled and sliced thin
2 shallots, peeled and sliced thin
2 bay leaves
1 cup white wine
1 teaspoon champagne vinegar
½ teaspoon crushed red pepper
1 medium Russet potato, peeled
6 whole thyme sprigs
4¼ cups clam broth
Extra virgin olive oil
1 teaspoon picked thyme leaves
Salt and black pepper

Cod
1 pound center cut cod loin, in 8 pieces
1 tablespoon canola oil
Salt and black pepper

Pan-Seared Maine Cod with Potato Broth and Oyster Crackers

> **And, yes, at the end of the day you still have to feed people real food.**

Spiced Lamb Loin with Carrot Purée, Olive-Raisin Compote and Tempura Clementine

Braised Oxtails

This recipe starts on the stovetop but can be finished either in the oven or in a crockpot. If finishing in the oven, preheat to 300°F and use a dutch oven or enameled cast iron pan. Season oxtail with salt and pepper then toss in flour until lightly coated. Start pan over high heat on the stovetop, add half the canola oil, turn down to medium and fry oxtails until golden brown on both sides, adding oil to pan as needed. Remove oxtails from pan. Drain all but 2 tablespoons of the oil then add carrots, celery and onion over medium high heat. Sauté until brown. Add tomato paste and stir until vegetables are evenly coated. Add wine and scrape up browned bits with wooden spoon. Reduce the liquid to a syrupy consistency. Add stock, bay leaves, herbs, allspice, balsamic, mustard, sugar, and oxtail and bring to a slow boil. Oven: Place pan in a 300°F preheated oven uncovered for approximately 3 hours or overnight at 200°F. Crockpot: cook in a covered crock pot about 8 hours on low or until meat is falling off the bone. Remove from the oven and let cool in liquid for at least 10 minutes or unplug crock pot and let sit for 10 minutes. Pull oxtail from liquid. Strain braising liquid, saving the vegetables to eat with oxtails but discarding spices. Reduce liquid in a sauce pan if it is too watery. Reheat vegetables and oxtail in a low oven and serve with sauce over your favorite starch and little coarse sea salt to taste. Short ribs, veal shank, lamb shank, and beef cheeks are all good substitutes for oxtails.

Serves 4-6

Ingredients

3 pounds oxtail
1 carrot, in 1" pieces
1 onion, chopped
2 celery stalks, in 1" pieces
1 tablespoon tomato paste
1 cup dry red wine
2 quarts chicken stock or water
2 tablespoons balsamic vinegar
2 whole bay leaves
½ cup canola oil
1 cup all purpose flour
1 teaspoon ground allspice
3 sprigs fresh thyme or sage
1 teaspoon grainy mustard
3 tablespoons sugar
Salt and pepper to taste

Braised Oxtails

Old Port Sea Grill

If you're looking for what sets the Old Port Sea Grill apart from every other Commercial Street restaurant, you could start with the magnificent bar. Long, curving, tinted concrete, it stretches the length of the building in a raised area separated from the floor by etched glass and blond wood panels.

At one end of the bar is another distinguishing feature, a deep well of crushed ice on which lie the oysters available that day, their names, exotic and local, listed on the slate hanging overhead.

"Between the bar and the oysters, we draw a crowd," says General Manager Drew Seaman with a laugh, "young professionals maybe having one of our fun cocktails or a bottle of wine, a couple of racks of oysters or small plates shared with a bunch of friends after work. There aren't many other restaurants that have 55 seats just in the bar. But then, later, they can go down and have a more intimate dinner in the dining room if they're looking for the same energy but a little less volume."

Those oysters—Flying Points from Freeport, Gliddens from Damariscotta, and Winterpoints from Bath in their seasons—are delivered direct from the producers, carefully washed, then bedded on constantly replenished crushed ice. "They're so fresh," adds Seaman, "because we take such good care of them and because they don't hang around. We go through 400 to 500 on a busy night."

Owner Laura Argitis points out that, with renowned seafood supplier Harbor Fish less than 500 feet away, "all the seafood we get is incredibly fresh, and so much of it is from right here, the Gulf of Maine, which makes the time from catch to plate that much shorter."

On the menu, Chef Chad Souders mixes traditional Maine offerings—fried clams, chowders, baked haddock, steamed lobster—with more exotic dishes marked by Asian, Italian, and other influences. "The Sea Grill serves all kinds of wood-grilled seafood," Argitis explains, "pork, steak, and chicken dishes for non-seafood eaters, but then always a couple specials where Chad can take something seasonal, halibut or cod, and be creative with it."

 You have to cook with all your senses," he continues, "where you can smell how something is going to taste way before it gets to your mouth.

Chef Chad Souders

Chef Souders at a Glance

Where do you find your inspiration?

Food shows, magazines, you get ideas for new preparations and ingredients.

Do you have any chef heroes?

Thomas Keller and Mario Batali, the classical and the rustic.

Do you have a spice mixture or flavor profile that pleases you?

The bright spicy Szechuan side of Asian food, chili garlic paste, fresh ginger.

Do you have a book that recently inspired you?

Anthony Bourdain's *The Nasty Bits*. All chefs should read his books.

Do you have a favorite country to travel to?

Italy, especially Venice for the seafood.

Spicy Creole Haddock and Corn Cakes with Remoulade

For the haddock cakes: preheat oven to 450°F. Cut the corn off the cob, toss in 1 tablespoon olive oil and roast in a small pan in the preheated oven for 30 minutes until nicely browned. Let the corn cool. Set aside. Sauté onion, pepper, and jalapeno in a pan with 2 tablespoons of the olive oil over medium heat until tender but not browned, about 10 minutes. Set aside and let cool. In a stock pot, combine the bay leaves, salt, peppercorns, Old Bay, and lemons and fill pot ¾ full of water. Bring the mixture to a boil. Put the diced haddock pieces into a metal strainer and lower strainer into the boiling liquid. Cook for approximately 5 minutes. Set haddock aside to let cool.

Combine the corn, onions, peppers, jalapeno, and haddock with one egg, mayonnaise and Cajun seasoning in a large bowl. Add ½ cup of the panko crumbs to the mixture and combine. If mixture does not hold when pressed together, mix in more panko crumbs 2 tablespoons at a time until mixture can hold. To dredge the cakes, place the remaining panko crumbs in a large bowl. Tightly pack a ¼ cup measure with the haddock mixture and roll into a ball in your hands. Press down to form a round cake about ¾ inches thick. Dredge in panko crumbs on all sides.

Heat 2 tablespoons of olive oil in a large skillet over medium-high heat. Add haddock cakes and sauté until golden brown, about 4 minutes per side, careful not to overcrowd the pan (you will have to do them in batches). Transfer to plates. Drizzle remoulade sauce over and serve.

For the roasted garlic and tomato remoulade: preheat oven to 450°F. Halve the tomatoes and using a spoon or melon baller, remove seeds and discard. Peel and halve the garlic cloves, put one inside each tomato half, and drizzle with the olive oil. Roast for 30 minutes or until the tomatoes and garlic are slightly charred. Add the remaining ingredients to a food processor or blender along with the tomatoes and garlic mixture. Pulse until everything is incorporated. Finish with salt and pepper to taste. Yield: approximately 1½ cups. Can be made a day ahead and refrigerated

Note: You can roast the tomatoes and garlic for the remoulade at the same time you roast the corn. Also, for less spicy cakes, use half of a pepper or omit half the Cajun seasoning.

Serves 6 as appetizer, 4 as entrée

Ingredients

Haddock and Corn Cakes

1 ear of corn, shucked
5 tablespoons olive oil
¼ cup large red onion, finely diced
¼ cup red peppers, finely diced
1 jalapeno pepper, seeded and finely diced
¾ pound fresh haddock, cut into 1" cubes
2 bay leaves
1 tablespoon salt
1 tablespoon whole black peppercorns
1 tablespoon Old Bay seasoning
2 lemons, halved
1 egg
½ cup mayonnaise
1 tablespoon Cajun seasoning
2 cups panko (Japanese bread crumbs)

Roasted Garlic and Tomato Remoulade

4 Roma tomatoes
8 garlic cloves
2 tablespoons olive oil
¾ cup mayonnaise
¼ cup capers
1 cup parsley leaves
Juice of ½ lemon
salt and pepper to taste

Spicy Creole Haddock and Corn Cakes with Remoulade

One winter offering, a wood-grilled Atlantic salmon fillet with wasabi mash, steamed baby bok choy and carrots in a soy-orange reduction, is a good example of his approach. "I'm giving people a beautiful piece of fish cooked over coals," Souders explains. "They know what the potatoes are but the wasabi's interesting, and then the bok choy, with the familiar carrots and then the orange-soy reduction, it's a little nudge to developing their palates. If they like to cook, they might find some approachable ideas here to take home."

"You have to cook with all your senses," he continues, "where you can smell how something is going to taste way before it gets to your mouth. Same way with your eyes. You're pan-roasting cod and you get a nice golden crust, you see that and say, hey, that caramelized flavor outside then the delicate flakiness of the fish when they bite into it, wow!" He shrugs. "Ultimate freshness, good quality ingredients, done approachably but with a few surprises to keep things interesting— that's how I like to cook."

Right: Fresh Oysters with trio of garnishes

Cod with Maple Sweet Potatoes & Roasted Brussels Sprouts

For the Brussels sprouts and bacon: remove the outer leaves and chop off the stem at the bottom of the sprout. Slice in half lengthwise. Next, fill a large bowl with ice and water and set aside. Bring a large pot of heavily salted water to a boil, add sprouts, and blanch 1-2 minutes. Remove the sprouts and place in the ice water bowl. Let the brussel sprouts cool completely, remove them from the ice water and place on kitchen towel to dry. While the sprouts are drying, add the diced bacon to a large skillet with 1 tablespoon olive oil over medium high heat. Once the bacon begins to render its fat, add the Brussels sprouts, salt and pepper and give the pan a quick toss. Place the skillet in the preheated oven and roast for 15-20 minutes.

For the sweet potatoes: while the sprouts roast, boil the sweet potatoes in a large pot of water for 20 minutes or until tender. Melt the butter. Drain the sweet potatoes and put them back into the pot. Using a masher, mash the potatoes, adding the maple syrup and warm melted butter. Salt and pepper to taste. Keep warm.

For the cod: preheat oven to 450°F. Salt and pepper both sides of the cod fillets and heat 2 tablespoons of olive oil in a large sauté pan over medium high heat. Once the oil is hot, sear the cod on one side for about 2 minutes, until a nice golden brown color. Flip the cod and place the pan in the preheated oven for 6-7 minutes. To serve, remove the cod from the oven. Place the mashed sweet potatoes and Brussels sprouts on the plate. Top with the cod.

Serves 4-6

Ingredients

4 7-8 ounce fresh cod fillets
1½ lbs of Brussels sprouts
4-5 slices of bacon, diced
3 large sweet potatoes, diced
3 tablespoons Maine maple syrup
8 ounces (1 stick) unsalted butter, melted
Salt and pepper to taste

Cod with Maple Sweet Potatoes & Roasted Brussels Sprouts

Mid-Maine

Yarmouth to Camden

Above: Cooks on the line at the Broad Arrow Tavern - Harraseeket Inn
Below: Chef Chris Bassett - Azure Café

Above: Chef Stephanie Brown and her assistant, Isaac Olson - Seagrass Bistro

Seagrass Bistro

Like every very good chef, Stephanie Brown, sole owner of Seagrass Bistro, is constantly looking over the reservation list a few days ahead. While the numbers may guide her ordering, it is the names that truly interest her.

"To me," she says, "feeding someone is probably the most intimate experience of *any* kind of work. In your first ten minutes at my restaurant table, I have the power to appeal to every single one of your senses—to your sight, your touch, your smell, your taste. Even the sizzle of the food as it comes to the table helps shape your experience. That is so powerful, and I take that responsibility very seriously."

The names are important to her because, while ever more new faces discover Seagrass in summer and other seasons, it is her regular clientele that sustains her, many who've been coming in most of the five years she's been open.

"I know where you like to sit," she laughs, "your food allergies, even if you're entertaining and might want a special from a previous menu. If there's going to be nothing on the menu you like that night, I will bring something in."

An Irish-Italian with deep North End roots—and a dazzling smile, Stephanie's ideas about food are equally down-to-earth. "Sometimes it seems as if people think they should go out and eat what the chef tells them to eat. My approach is, just tell me what you'd like to eat, and I'll figure out how best to cook it for you."

She serves American bistro-style cuisine with Asian, French, and Italian influences. French from her culinary background, Asian for its lightness, "that sesame, soy, spice flare that is so great for vegetarian and summer dishes," she says. "Italian is my roots, home-cooked meals everybody can relate to."

From late April through Thanksgiving, most of her produce comes from New Leaf Farm just next door in Durham, "unbelievable greens and vegetables that come through the door almost every day." Her seafood and meats are also as local as can be.

The menu changes every three weeks, driven in season by what the farmers harvest. "People say 'Your food tastes so good, so fresh,'" she says. "I want to tell them, of course! It was picked or caught yesterday and on your plate today, not chilled or frozen and sitting in a crate on a truck or plane for a week just to get here. And of course, I made it for you!"

Not many restaurants change their menus with such frequency, but it is part of Stephanie's almost Zen approach to her art. "We take a week to create the menu and perfect it," she says thoughtfully, "a week to embrace it, then a week to totally get into its rhythm, enjoy it. At the end of every day," she continues, "I clean the stoves and counters and wipe away all the stresses. Regardless of how hard the day, I leave it behind to come in the next morning and have everything new and different. That's just one reason I really love my work."

Chef Stephanie Brown and her assistant, Isaac Olson

Chef Brown at a Glance

Where do you find your inspiration?

My friends and family inspire me a lot, they're my support system.

Do you have any chef heroes?

Jody Adams at Rialto in Cambridge, Massachusetts.

What book has recently inspired you?

Becoming A Chef by Andrew Dornenburg and Karen Page.

Do you have a favorite kitchen implement?

My fish spatula, my absolute favorite, I use it for everything.

What's your favorite cheese?

Cotswold cheese, from England.

Marinated Grilled Mushroom Salad with Endive

In a medium bowl, place mustard, 2 tablespoons of the vinegar, garlic, thyme, salt, pepper and whisk into a thick paste. Very slowly drizzle oil while whisking to form a full thick emulsion. A blender may also be used instead of a whisk.

Put 1 cup of balsamic vinegar in a 1-quart sauce pan and reduce on medium heat until thickened to a syrup.

Wipe any dirt off the mushrooms with a dry towel and then place in vinaigrette. Let sit for 15 minutes and then place on hot grill or under the broiler, tossing frequently to grill all sides.

To assemble the salad, first separate and clean the endive leaves. Divide the mushrooms between four plates, garnish with the endive, then use a carrot peeler to shave the Pecorino for topping. Lastly, drizzle balsamic reduction over each salad and serve.

Serves 4

Ingredients

2 cups crimini mushrooms
3 tablespoon whole grain mustard
1 cup + 2 tablespoons balsamic vinegar
2 cloves garlic, lightly crushed and peeled
2 sprigs fresh thyme
Kosher salt and fresh ground pepper to
  taste
¾ cup light olive oil
1 head Belgian endive leaves
Pecorino Romano cheese for shaving

Marinated Grilled Mushroom Salad with Endive

> *To me, she says, feeding someone is probably the most intimate experience of any kind of work. In your first ten minutes at my restaurant table, I have the power to appeal to every single one of your senses—to your sight, your touch, your smell, your taste.*

Grilled Maple Bourbon Shrimp with Sweet Rum Pineapple

Panko Crusted Chicken Cutlets with Tomato Reduction

For the chicken: preheat oven to 375°F. Trim any excess fat or bone scraps from chicken breasts. Dry with paper towel and then cut the chicken in three thin slices horizontally to form a cutlet. Some breasts may yield 4 slices.

Put the flour in the bottom of a large shallow bowl. Beat the eggs lightly in another bowl. Put the panko in a third, large bowl. Dredge chicken in flour, then egg, followed by panko bread crumbs. Place on cookie sheet sprayed with nonstick spray and drizzle each cutlet with oil. Season with salt & pepper. Bake for 30 minutes or until golden brown.

For the reduction: lightly crush garlic and peel. Gently heat extra virgin olive oil in a sauce pan with the garlic. Let garlic simmer in oil until golden brown. Turn off heat and gently pour tomatoes in oil. Resume heat and let simmer for 20 minutes. Season with salt & pepper to taste. Let cool and then blend until smooth. Return to simmer to heat at serving.

Place a small ladleful of sauce on bottom of warmed plates, add wilted greens of your choice, and place golden cutlets atop greens. Garnish with fresh basil and Pecorino shavings made with a carrot peeler.

Serves 6

Chicken

3 boneless chicken breasts
4 eggs
1 cup flour
1 pound panko (Japanese bread crumbs)
Nonstick spray
Light olive oil for drizzling
Kosher salt and pepper

Reduction

3 large garlic cloves
¼ cup Spanish extra virgin olive oil
1 16-ounce can whole peeled tomatoes
Kosher salt and fresh ground pepper to taste
½ cup basil leaves, torn
Shaved Pecorino Romano to garnish

Panko Crusted Chicken Cutlets with Tomato Reduction

Azure Café

When Jonas Werner and his wife, Kate, who grew up in Maine, moved to Freeport from Portland eight years ago, it was not just because they had found a good place to open a restaurant. "We were hoping to find a great sense of community," Jonas recalls, "and to be more in touch with our natural surroundings, and to have

Executive Chef Chris Bassett

that reflected in the food, its quality and preparation, too."

At the Azure Café just a block from LLBean, they have found all that and more, creating an oasis that welcomes the locals and summer visitors with a menu divided into comfort food they call "Azure Classics" on the one hand, and "A Taste of Italy" on the other.

"The dishes on our menu," says Executive Chef Chris Bassett, "are so simple and pleasing that people get it right away, even the more adventurous things for those who like to experiment."

"Our focus is above all to make people feel comfortable," Jonas adds, "but remind them of a trip to Italy, or their *nonna's* cooking, too, which is just the best kind of compliment we can get."

Out on a double date? One diner can take comfort in a haddock stuffed with Maine shrimp, scallops, and crab – and the breadcrumbs on the *inside*, "so you can really taste the fresh fish, too," Chef Bassett insists—while another dives into a Marsala orange-glazed duck breast served with pancetta and butternut squash risotto over wilted beet greens. The other two might be venturing into more squarely Italian dishes, homemade pastas and meats and seafoods sauced with ingredients from the network of farms that supplies Azure.

"I sometimes joke," says Jonas, "that the most important thing we can do here is try to get God's work to the table without screwing it up. So much of what makes food good is already in it before it gets to the kitchen. It's our job to just bring those flavors and textures together in the right way."

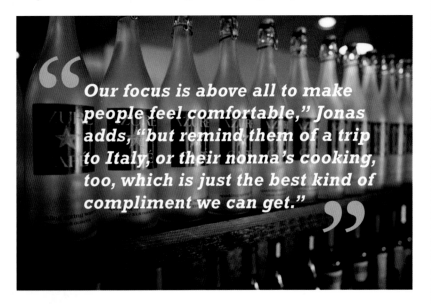

" *Our focus is above all to make people feel comfortable," Jonas adds, "but remind them of a trip to Italy, or their nonna's cooking, too, which is just the best kind of compliment we can get."* "

Chef Bassett at a Glance

Do you have any chef heroes?

Michel Richard and Charlie Trotter.

When you're not cooking, what do you do to relax?

I'm an avid cyclist, mountain biking, road cycling, and BMX stunt riding, and I'm highly involved in the Maine Roller Derby scene, as the head referee for the league.

Is there a country whose cuisine is particularly undervalued?

The United States. Our cuisine has been defined for twenty years.

Is there a book that has recently inspired you?

Michel Richard's *Happy in the Kitchen: The Craft of Cooking, The Art of Eating.*

What's your favorite cheese?

York Hill Vegetable Ash Aged Goat Cheese.

Green Leaf Salad with Goat Cheese and Maple Vinaigrette

Sometimes, the simplest of combinations can be more interesting to the palate than the most complicated. Here, creamy chèvre, the slight crunch of the berries and fresh greens, and the tangy zest of maple and cider work to make a very light but satisfying first course.

The vinaigrette can been made by hand with a whisk, but, for best results, use a small handheld immersion blender.

For the vinaigrette: combine thyme, shallots, maple, vinegar, salt, pepper and Cayenne pepper in a tall, narrow, cylindrical container (or small bowl if whisking by hand). Blend ingredients well, then slowly add olive oil to form an emulsion.

Portion greens, raspberries, and chèvre and toss in 4 shallow salad bowls. Dress with vinaigrette at room temperature. If vinaigrette separates, whisk before serving.

Serves 4

Ingredients

6 cups mixed baby greens, washed
1 cup red raspberries, washed
4 ounces plain chèvre goat cheese, crumbled or in 4 slices, as desired
1½ teaspoons shallot, finely minced
½ teaspoon fresh thyme, leaves minced
¼ cup Maine maple syrup
3 tablespoons apple cider vinegar
½ teaspoon Maine sea salt
¼ teaspoon freshly ground black pepper
¼ teaspoon Cayenne pepper
½ cup olive oil

Green Leaf Salad with Fresh Raspberries, Goat Cheese and Spicy Maple Vinaigrette

The space itself is divided into a small bar and relaxed, open-plan area with widely-spaced tables on the first floor and a more private venue upstairs. Out front, a flower-decked stone patio welcomes the guest into a lively bustle of people from all over the country and the world enjoying the food and ambiance under the ancient trees that tower over it.

Along with the thoughtful food and great atmosphere, the Azure Café rounds out the experience with fun and funky seasonal cocktails, and a wine selection praised by Wine Spectator magazine. This is only possible, again, because Jonas cares enough to put his young wines aside until "they are really at the peak," as he puts it, "the full expression of what they should be, not hurried along and served willy-nilly with the hope that they will be mature."

"What we do is pretty simple," Jonas sums up. "We don't feed egos, either our own or the chefs', we just feed people."

Crema Caramella with Toasted Pine Nuts

Scallops in Vermouth with Mushroom Couscous "Risotto"

Couscous: in a 3-4 quart, heavy-bottomed saucepan, sauté the onions in the olive oil over medium-high heat. When onions start to brown, add garlic, stir for 1 minute then add water, couscous, and sea salt. Bring to a boil, then reduce to a simmer and cover. Simmer 10 minutes, remove from heat, and stir gently to keep couscous from clumping. Set aside.

Mushroom "risotto": preheat large sauté pan over medium-high heat. Melt butter in pan and sauté onions, garlic, and mushrooms until they start to brown around the edges. Add cream and salt. Bring to a boil, add couscous, breaking up any clumps. Cook until most of the cream has soaked into mixture. Remove from heat and, reserving a bit of each for garnish, gently fold in parsley and chives. Adjust salt and pepper.

Scallops: preheat medium sauté pan over high heat. Once hot, add oil, and immediately and carefully place scallops in pan with a flat side down. Sear only one side until you can see a light brown caramelization coming up the sides. Remove from heat and add vermouth. Gently remove scallops, one by one, and place them seared side up in a room temperature casserole dish. Add cream to sauté pan with vermouth and return to high heat. Bring to a boil then immediately pour over scallops in casserole dish. Let rest for 2-3 minutes. (The hot cream will finish cooking the scallops.) Season the sauce to taste with salt and pepper. To serve, portion risotto equally in 4 large bowls, divide scallops and place around risotto, pour 2-3 tablespoons of sauce over the scallops, and garnish with reserved parsley and chives.

Serves 4

Ingredients

Couscous

2 tablespoons olive oil
2 tablespoons yellow onion, finely diced
1 teaspoon garlic, minced
1 cup Israeli couscous
1¼ cups water
2 teaspoons Maine sea salt

Mushroom "Risotto"

1 tablespoon unsalted butter
4 tablespoons yellow onion, finely diced
4 teaspoons garlic, minced
2 cups oyster mushrooms, cut in ½"
    pieces
1 cup heavy cream
2 teaspoons Maine sea salt
Prepared couscous
2 tablespoons parsley, chopped
2 tablespoons chives, chopped

Scallops and Sauce

1 tablespoon canola oil
1½ pounds medium Maine sea scallops
½ cup sweet Vermouth
1 cup heavy cream

Scallops in Vermouth with Mushroom Couscous "Risotto"

77

The Harraseeket Inn
Maine Dining Room and Broad Arrow Tavern

What do a 27-foot-long walk-in refrigerator overflowing with Maine bounty from land and sea, a five-course lobster tasting menu, a wood-fired oven, Chateaubriand served tableside—and a stuffed moose head—have

in common? They all are part of the refreshing and far-ranging approach the culinary team at the Harraseeket Inn has brought to dining there.

When the Gray family started the Inn over 25 years ago as a five-room B & B, it hardly had one kitchen, much less the two restaurants it boasts today, the grand Maine Dining Room and the open, more casual Broad Arrow Tavern.

"There's not much here that we haven't changed over the years," Nancy Gray says of the Inn's growth from five to over 90 rooms in an elegant old-timey building on the main street, "but there's a lot that has stayed the same, too."

Executive Chef Theda Lyden (center)

Executive Chef Theda Lyden, who has worked with Mrs. Gray for so long that the two often finish each other's sentences, is quick to point out that this marriage of old and new carries over from the facilities to the thinking behind the food. Like that Chateaubriand in the Maine Dining Room. "Mrs. Gray wanted to give people an experience that *is* a lost art," Chef Lyden says, "and so we do tableside service for Chateaubriand, rack of lamb, Caesar Salads, and dessert soufflés. It makes the whole room festive, dramatic, a place where you can come and celebrate."

Such quality goes back to the ingredients, of course, which is why the Inn has relationships which have endured through thick and thin with more than 30 farmers and purveyors of every kind of vegetable and fruit to free-range chickens, lobsters, and shellfish. With recent low lobster prices and poor summer farm weather, the kitchen staff has taken on the challenge of helping their friends through tough times. "We've been using a lot of lobster," Mrs. Gray explains, "because the guys need to sell it." "The guys" are the Merrymans of Potts Harbor, and they've been delivering fresh lobster daily to the inn for more than fifteen years. "Our five-course lobster tasting menu came about because of the plight of the lobstermen," Lyden adds. "A lobster stew, a lobster crêpe, a lobster spring roll, a lobster risotto, and a lazy man's lobster over fresh pasta, easily a pound of meat in there."

Chef Lyden at a Glance

Do you have any chef heroes?

It would be hard not to say Alice Waters.

Where do you find inspiration?

In nature. I'm an avid gardener, and I like to grow foods based on their flavor.

What book has influenced you lately?

I just finished Nicole Mones' *The Last Chinese Chef*, and I loved it.

Do you have a favorite cheese?

York Hill Farm Capriano goat cheese.

When you're not cooking, what do you do to relax?

I am an artist, a potter, I have a clay studio.

What country's cuisine do you find most underrated?

Traveling in Eastern Europe last year, the food of Vienna really impressed me.

Fettuccine all'Aragosta (Lobster Fettuccine)

Make a broth with the lobster bodies: chop bodies into small pieces and put into stockpot together with onion, celery, carrot, and enough water to cover them. Simmer 30 minutes, discard solids, reduce liquid to 2 cups. Reserve.

In a shallow saucepan, heat 3 tablespoons butter and the olive oil over medium heat. Add leek, shallot, and a pinch of salt, and sweat them until translucent, about 5 minutes. Add tomatoes and cook until they soften, then add cream sherry, cooking until the alcohol has evaporated, about 3 minutes. Stir in tomato paste, lobster broth, lemon juice, and cream. Continue cooking until sauce is thick enough to coat the back of a spoon then reduce to low heat. Finish the sauce by stirring in the last 2 tablespoons of butter and the lobster meat, chopped or in large pieces as preferred.

Cook the pasta in plenty of salted water, drain, reserve 1 cup of the water to add to the sauce as needed if it is too thick. Add the pasta to the lobster sauce, tossing to coat, garnish with fennel fronds if desired.

Serves 4

Ingredients

2 lobsters, cooked and picked, bodies
  reserved
1 small onion, roughly chopped
1 carrot, roughly chopped
1 stalk celery, roughly chopped
4 cups+ cold water
8 ounces fresh fettuccine (or linguini)
1 shallot, finely diced
½ pint grape or cherry tomatoes, halved
½ medium leek, thinly sliced
Fennel fronds (optional)
3 tablespoons tomato paste
¼ cup cream sherry
2 cups lobster broth (or fish stock)
¾ cup heavy cream
Juice of ½ lemon
5 tablespoons unsalted butter
2 tablespoons olive oil
Salt

Fettuccine all'Aragosta (Lobster Fettuccine)

"

*We have so many people coming from away
who want to experience Maine, and this is just
one of the ways they get to do it, by eating the
very best that our state produces . . .*

Stout and Chili Braised Short Ribs over Parmesan Polenta

Rehydrate the chilis by putting them in a small bowl and pouring boiling water over them. Let sit 15 minutes then drain. Meanwhile, in a heavy-bottomed pan, sear the ribs in their own fat until browned on all sides. Put the drained chilis and one bottle of stout in a blender and mix until smooth. Pour this mixture over the ribs, add the remaining stout and beef broth, cover, and simmer on low 4 hours or until ribs are fork tender.

For the polenta, bring the stock to a slow boil in a saucepan and whisk in polenta bit by bit. Cook on low heat, stirring frequently, until polenta comes away cleanly from the sides of the pan, about 30 minutes. Mix in cheese and butter and pour into a greased 9"X9" baking pan to set. Let cool. Refrigerate at least two hours.

To serve, cut polenta into 4 squares and sear in the oil in a cast-iron or heavy pan. Serve each square smothered in the ribs and braising liquid.

Serves 4

Ingredients

Ribs

2 pounds boneless beef short ribs
2 12-ounce bottles Gritty's Black Fly Stout
5-7 dried New Mexico red chilis (also called chile de ristra)
16 ounces beef stock

Polenta

4 cups chicken stock
1 cup polenta
4 tablespoons unsalted butter
½ cup grated parmesan
1 tablespoon canola oil
Salt and pepper to taste

Stout and Chili Braised Short Ribs over Parmesan Polenta

Above: Broad Arrow Tavern

This food is mirrored in a very different but just as embracing way in the warm and welcoming Broad Arrow Tavern with its fireplace, roaring wood-fired oven and grill and scurrying chefs at work right in front of the guests. At first glance, the rustic hunting lodge décor seems to be directly inspired by L.L.Bean just down the street—until you learn that three generations of Mrs. Gray's family have been innkeepers and the inspiration came from her youth growing up in a remote sporting camp near Jackman.

"When we did the Tavern," Mrs. Gray says, "we designed it to look like Birch Island Lodge, with the moose head and the bear and the deer. People like that it looks like a Maine sporting camp."

"Both of our restaurants have a lot of energy," Chef Lyden finishes, "but each is a different energy, and a different menu. We have so many people coming from away who want to experience Maine, and this is just one of the ways they get to do it, by eating the very best that our state produces."

Of course, what Gray, Chef Lyden and the entire staff are all too modest to point out is that staying at the Harraseeket and eating there is a premiere Maine experience that embraces you from the moment you step through the door.

White Chocolate Cherry Tuile Napoleon

For the tuiles: preheat the oven to 325°F. In a large bowl mix together all tuile ingredients. Do not beat. Drop by the rounded teaspoonful onto greased parchment paper or greased nonstick cookie sheet, spreading each mound into a thin circle about 2 ½" in diameter. Bake until edges are golden and let cool completely before moving.

For the Mousse: first whip the heavy cream until it stands in thick peaks and set aside. Put the milk in a small saucepan then add the gelatin, letting it sit until the gelatin expands and disappears. Bring the milk mixture to a boil, remove from heat. Pour the milk into the bowl of a food processor and add white chocolate, processing until smooth. Add the salt, oil, and vanilla. Transfer this to a large mixing bowl and let it cool 5 minutes before folding in whipped cream. Refrigerate overnight.

Cherry sauce: combine the cherries, sugar, and water in a small saucepan and bring to a boil. Simmer until the consistency of a thick sauce. Cool.

Assembly: put a tuile on each dessert plate, spoon on a layer of the mousse, and dot with a few cherries. Repeat twice more, and garnish with the last of the sauce.

Serves 4-6

Ingredients

Oatmeal Lace Tuiles
1½ cups oatmeal
1½ cups brown sugar
2 tablespoons flour
½ teaspoon salt
1¼ sticks unsalted butter, melted
1 egg
½ teaspoon vanilla

White Chocolate Mousse
½ pound Ghirardelli white chocolate
⅓ cup milk
1 tablespoon powdered gelatin
1 pinch salt
2 tablespoons vegetable oil
1 tablespoon vanilla
2 cups heavy cream

Cherry Sauce
1 cup fresh or frozen sour cherries
1 cup sugar
2 tablespoons water

White Chocolate Cherry Tuile Napoleon

Above: Chefs Daphne Comaskey & Eloise Humphrey - El Camino
Below: Chef Tyne Sansom - Solo Bistro

Above: Chef Brian Hill - Francine Bistro
Below: Chef Paul Landry - Fishbones American Grill

El Camino Cantina

Imagine a restaurant—authentic, serious CalMex cuisine, mostly organic, farmer-driven, very affordable and run by twin sisters with a penchant for vintage duds and eye-popping color schemes. Oh, and with a bar so good its Margarita was picked best in the US by GQ a few years back….this must be Berkeley or Boston, right? Nope!

Since Paul and Daphne Comaskey, and Daphne's sister, Eloise Humphrey, hit town 6 years ago, Brunswick has never been the same. In their restaurant, El Camino Cantina, against a backdrop half Tijuana roadhouse and half hip saloon, the magic flows five nights a week with cocktail specials and a compact menu driven by an emphasis on local and seasonal. Paul's is the first face you'll see as he juggles a full room of diners waiting for tables and takes the edge off your hunger with an equal mix of drinks, house salsa and guacamole, and Irish humor.

Chefs Daphne Comaskey & Eloise Humphrey

Whether you are vegetarian or carnivore, there is always something on the nightly Specials board to fill the belly and let you feel good doing it. Far less than $20 gets you a plate of quesadillas, nachos, soft tacos, or salads bursting with organic meat and poultry, or Maine shrimp, fish, or scallops, or a bevy of seasonal vegetables garnished with salsas and molés and local cheeses, nearly every ingredient provided by one of 25 local producers.

And it's not just the food on the plates that's local, either. "We've done catering for Presidents and Coppollas and worked in high end restaurants in New York, San Francisco, and we just got tired of that," Eloise says. "We wanted to make a restaurant," her sister adds, "where the farmers can eat, but with the same high quality of local ingredients lovingly prepared for a wide audience."

Over sixty years of shared restaurant experience gives them a deep well to draw on for inspiration, but the twin phenomenon also helps—that complementariness of Eloise the wild cheffie creative type pondering whether the perfect spring soup should be green garlic or fresh pea, while Daph can take down 25 chickens, throw together the tomatillo salsa, and watch over twelve racks of roasting vegetables all at the same time.

> ***We wanted to show that you could have good food, a lot of it organic and all natural, but in Maine, where people don't have that much money.***

Chef Humphrey at a Glance

Do you have any chef heroes?

Diana Kennedy, Rick Bayless, and, when I was really young, Alice Waters.

What book has influenced you lately?

Zarela Martinez's *The Food and Life of Oaxaca*.

Do you have a favorite cheese?

Anything from Hahn's End, in Phippsburg.

What kind of a knife do you use?

My favorites I bought in Paris when I was 18, two wooden-handled knives that I've had more than half my life.

Do you have a kitchen utensil that is particularly pleasing to you?

I love wooden pepper grinders, the shape of them, and the microplane.

Corn Soup with Cilantro-Pumpkin Seed Pesto

A light, summery start to a meal in any season.

Make a corn stock by putting cobs, cilantro stems, and the halved jalapeño into 4 quart saucepan and adding water to cover, at least 2 quarts. Bring to boil, turn heat to low and simmer 20 minutes. Strain and reserve.

Prepare pesto by puréeing cilantro tops, pumpkin seeds, lime juice, half jalapeño, and salt in a food processor. Scrape down the sides of the bowl. With processor running, add oil in a thin stream until thoroughly incorporated. Adjust salt for seasoning.

For the soup, first heat the butter or oil in a four-quart, heavy-bottomed saucepan on medium. Add onion and cook over low for 5 minutes or until translucent. Add 6 cups corn stock and reserved corn kernels. Gently simmer for 10 minutes. Remove from heat and purée with immersion blender. Strain soup through a fine mesh sieve pushing on solids with the bottom of a ladle. Add salt to taste and more stock to preferred consistency. Return to pot if serving immediately or allow to cool before refrigerating. Warm soup and garnish with the pesto before serving.

Serves 4-6

Ingredients

Corn Soup

2 tablespoons butter or canola oil
1 medium sweet onion, diced, about ¾ cup
8 ears freshest sweet corn, kernels cut off
   and cobs reserved
Salt to taste, about 2 teaspoons
About 2 quarts water
1 bunch cilantro, leaves plucked, about
   ¾ cup, and stems reserved
1 jalapeño pepper, halved

Cilantro-Pumpkin Seed Pesto

Reserved cilantro tops
½ cup toasted pumpkin seeds
1-2 teaspoons fresh lime juice
½ fresh jalapeño, seeded and chopped
½ teaspoon salt
¾ cup canola oil

Corn Soup with Cilantro-Pumpkin Seed Pesto

Above: Squash Soft Tacos

Good, long relationships with farmers, buying in quantity in season, and pickling, freezing, saucing, and otherwise preserving summer's bounty to enliven February's drear—these clever and traditional tricks are one more way they make the most of Maine's short growing season and keep the place affordable.

El Camino itself, its food and ambiance and horseshoe bar and wacky kitsch Mexican decor, the very good drinks and simple but so well conceived menu—it all looks so easy, as it does in any very good, well-run restaurant. Talk to the two about the effort that goes into the food, however, it becomes quite personal very quickly. As Eloise says, "We wanted to show that you could have good food, a lot of it organic and all natural, but in Maine, where people don't have that much money. Sometimes I think people have so much fun eating here they think we can't be serious about the food – until they taste it."

Pumpkin Caramel Flan

Maple and pumpkin put a Maine twist on this traditional Mexican dessert.

Preheat oven to 300 °F. Place custard cups in large (9in.x13in.) deep baking dish.

For the caramel: measure ¾ cup sugar into a small heavy saucepan. Stir in the water and bring to a boil. Wash down the sugar crystals that form on the sides of the pan with a pastry brush dipped in water and continue to boil until the mixture is light amber. Working carefully, pour evenly into the bottoms of the custard cups and set aside.

For the pumpkin custard: whisk the eggs in a large mixing bowl until well blended and set aside. Pour the milk, cream, pumpkin, 1/3 cup sugar, spices, and vanilla into a medium sauce pan and stir until combined. Bring to a simmer but do not boil.

Add the hot custard mixture gradually to the beaten eggs while whisking constantly. Strain this mixture through a fine meshed sieve into large measuring cup or pitcher with spout. Divide evenly among prepared custard cups. Surround the custard cups in the baking dish with boiling water until it reaches halfway up their sides and cover the whole tray lightly with foil. Carefully place in preheated oven. Bake until center of flan still has slight jiggle, about ½ hour. Remove cups from water bath with tongs and allow to cool before refrigerating. To serve: run knife around edge of mold, place plate on top and invert. Serve with whipped cream drizzled with maple syrup.

6 Individual Servings

Ingredients

¾ cup plus ⅓ cup sugar
½ cup water
1⅓ cup milk
½ cup heavy cream
4 large eggs
½ cup pumpkin purée
½ teaspoon ground cinnamon
⅛ teaspoon grated nutmeg
¼ teaspoon ground allspice
Pinch ground cloves
¼ teaspoon ground ginger
¼ teaspoon vanilla extract
1 cup whipped cream
Maple syrup

Pumpkin Caramel Flan

Solo Bistro

What people admire most about Bath is a New England authenticity that only a working shipyard, a storied riverfront, and a redbrick downtown nationally recognized for its historical distinctiveness can provide. Nestled into one such building on Front Street is a convivial place where the food is local, seasonal, and its flavors and preparation drawn from the same rich traditions. Will and Pia Neilson's award-winning Solo Bistro welcomes the visitor into a bright, lively refuge whose cozy downstairs wine bar and open plan main room– with only a half-wall separating the kitchen from many diners – bring a touch of casual modernity to this timeless setting.

Since their opening in 2005, the couple has worked hard to bring a new vibe to their part of Front Street, expanding the space and bringing in jazz on Friday nights and fixed price menus that "offer a good choice for everyone, as well as being an unbelievable value," Will notes. "One three-course menu is under $20," he adds. "Now people come from away and are astonished at what they get for the price. It's a bistro, and our aim is to offer uncompromising quality and superlative — though not necessarily fancy — food and drink in an informal place where you can always get a burger or a steak or some kind of fish but also something interesting and local."

Solo Bistro's not so well-kept secret is a congenial staff under Pia's competent and firm hand and an able, well-oiled kitchen plating up more contemporary, big-city flavors alongside gentle re-interpretations of regional classics. Chef Tyne Sansom is, Will says, "not limited to one cuisine at all. Solo Bistro's food is very American in the sense that it is very eclectic, both because of the region's ingredients and because we're not willing to limit ourselves that way."

Chef Tyne Sansom

"I'm classically French trained," says Chef Sansom, "but I've spent time in New Mexico and got introduced to southwestern cooking, then most recently I worked with an Italian cook who opened my eyes to traditional pasta-making and the Italian philosophy." What this means in practice is, for example, the Solo Bistro haddock. "It's stuffed with crab, sure," Sansom says, smiling, "but accented with green chile and beurre blanc, a fusion of New Mexico and French with a fresh Maine fish."

Their menu varies seasonally, but also changes weekly with specials conceived to satisfy both local appetites and summer visitors while using the Gulf of Maine's bounty of fish and shellfish and readily available organic produce from area farms. Will oversees the wine, building on his and Pia's extensive travels, particularly in Europe, which is why you'll find some happy surprises on the list. Surprisingly contemporary, too, would describe Pia's décor—Scandinavian flatware and crystal, Barcelona-designed chairs in a bright, modern style, the whole complemented by tasteful Angela Adams wall hangings.

"Part of what I love about this place *is* its traditional side," says Will, "but that it also welcomes things that are different, if at its own pace." And that pace, Will notes, is accelerating as the town is discovered by more and more visitors looking for something different, something Solo Bistro is happy to provide.

Chef Sansom at a Glance

Where do you find your inspiration?
Fresh local ingredients, the fresher the better.

What's your favorite cheese?
Black Diamond Five Year Cheddar.

Do you have any chef heroes?
Gordon Ramsay.

What do you do to relax?
Play with my sons, make and enjoy homebrewed beer.

Is there a country you like to travel to?
My birthplace, Fredericton, New Brunswick, Canada.

What's your favorite midnight snack?
Jalapeño jelly and cream cheese on crackers.

Pan Fried Mushrooms on Brioche Toast

For the brioche: dissolve sugar and yeast in warm milk and let sit for 5 minutes. In the bowl of a stand mixer, beat eggs and butter until combined. Add yeast mixture and beat until combined. Beat in flour and salt and continue beating for 5–10 minutes until dough is smooth and pliable. Oil a large, clean bowl lightly with vegetable oil, put the dough in the bowl, cover, and let rise till doubled in size, about 1 hour. Punch down and shape into a loaf. Place dough in a greased 9" X 4" loaf pan, cover and let rise until doubled, about 45 minutes. Preheat oven to 350°F. Bake bread for 35-40 minutes, till well browned on top and the bottom of the pan sounds hollow when tapped. Remove from pan immediately and cool on a wire rack. Cut four ½" thick slices when ready to serve.

For the mushrooms: reconstitute the morels in warm water then drain on paper towels. Clean, dry, then cut the oyster mushrooms off their stalks, slicing large mushrooms in half. Melt 2 tablespoons of butter in a large sauté pan and add the mushrooms, frying until golden brown. Add the Madeira, turn up the heat, toss the mushrooms, salt and pepper to taste, then keep warm. In another large, clean sauté pan, melt 1 tablespoon butter and toast the brioche until brown, add remaining butter and toast other side. Pour mushrooms on brioche and serve immediately.

Serves 4 as a light appetizer

Ingredients

Brioche
2¾ cups all purpose flour
3 tablespoons sugar
1½ teaspoon salt
2 teaspoons yeast
2 eggs
⅓ cup warm milk
½ cup unsalted butter, room temperature

Mushrooms
6 ounces king oyster mushrooms
2 ounces dried morels
4 tablespoons butter
2 tablespoons Madeira
Salt and black pepper

Pan Fried Mushrooms on Brioche Toast

> **Solo Bistro's food is very American in the sense that it is very eclectic, both because of the region's ingredients and because we're not willing to limit ourselves that way.**

Individual Melted Leek Tart

Seared Scallops with Artisanal Bacon and Wilted Arugula

At Solo Bistro, we make this classic but simple dish with our own applewood-smoked bacon, a surprisingly easy process given below for those who have a stovetop smoker.

For the scallops: slice the bacon and cook in large sauté pan until crispy. Drain on paper towel and set aside. Drain off all but 2 tablespoons of the bacon fat from the pan. Put the pan on high heat, then sear the scallops until golden brown, about 1 minute per side over high heat. Remove scallops, add the baby arugula to the pan, and toss over high heat with the lemon juice. On four plates, layer first the bacon slices, then the arugula and top with scallops. Serve with wedges of fresh lemon.

To make your own bacon: mix together salt, sugar and pickling spice. Rub pork belly with mixture until lightly coated (some salt mixture will be left over). Roll the belly tightly and tie with butchers twine. Hang it in a 5-gallon bucket for 9 days in a refrigerated place. Then, untie butchers twine and place belly in stovetop smoker with hickory or applewood chips. Smoke lightly for 40 minutes. Will keep, refrigerated, for two weeks.

Serves 4 as an appetizer

Ingredients

Scallops

1 pound Maine divers scallops
8 slices artisanal applewood-smoked
   bacon
2 cups baby arugula
2 tablespoons lemon juice
1 lemon cut into thin wedges

Homemade Bacon*

2 pounds pork belly, skin removed
½ cup kosher salt
½ cup sugar
2 tablespoons pickling spice
*Optional

Seared Scallops with Artisanal Bacon
and Wilted Arugula

Fishbones American Grill

At the old brick Bates Mill #6 in downtown Lewiston, Paul and Kate Landry have carved out a restaurant where the welcome is as easy and genuine as the food is comforting—and varied. You stroll into Fishbones American Grill to find a generous bar with ample stools facing sofas and armchairs, underfoot soft-toned etched cement

floors sprouting columns and rustic wooden beams, to one side a clubby private dining room, the other an open dining space. The whole ensemble, with attentive waitstaff in immediate attendance, draws you in right away, the air perfumed with rich smells promising a good time to come. The first-time visitor can be forgiven for thinking, as plate follows plate in the company of just the right wines, that he might have been transported to another, more cosmopolitan city altogether.

Part of the Landrys' success is in the simple logic of their goals. "We're not trying to be all things to all people," Paul says, "but instead to offer dishes that appeal to most — and what's more, that will arrive beautifully presented, perfectly cooked 100 times a night, every night."

"We're in the accommodation business, really," says Executive Chef David Moyse. "You want a special order—vegan or vegetarian, avoiding a food allergy, sauce on the side, raw plate, whatever—we can do that."

"And if you ask us to split an entrée," Paul finishes, "each of you gets the full presentation, all the sides and starches, not some pathetic thing marooned on the plate you're paying four bucks extra for."

Though fish is certainly on the menu, particularly specials featuring Atlantic species in season such as cod, halibut, and Maine shellfish delivered almost daily from the coast, the chefs here like to take more traditional dishes, "and give them the Fishbones touch," as David puts it.

Chef Paul Landry

Chef Landry at a Glance

Where do you find your inspiration?

I always go back to my old cookbooks for inspiration, Escoffier, Carême, because that's where it started for me.

What kind of knife do you use?

I have a 25-year-old Henckels, a 12" low profile, chef's knife that I love.

Do you have a spice mixture or flavor profile that pleases you?

I like the way rosemary, thyme, and sage work together, that's what we grow most of.

What country do you think has the most underrated food?

Italy, whose food is not all tomato sauce based as most Americans think.

What's your favorite cheese?

Vermont Butter and Cheese Company chèvre because it's not too salty.

You can bring your mémère," — what Lewiston's numerous Franco-Americans call their grandmothers — "you can bring your foodie friends, and they're all going to find something to eat in a really comfortable place and not walk out feeling hungry or robbed.

Seared Duck with Lentil Ragout and Dried Cherry Port Sauce

For the lentil ragout: simmer the lentils together with the thyme and rosemary sprigs, garlic cloves and chicken stock until the lentils are tender, about 15-20 minutes. Drain lentils over a bowl to reserve their cooking liquid, remove herbs and garlic cloves, set aside. In a saucepan, cook the diced bacon until almost crispy, add the shallots and sauté 10 seconds, then add the cooked lentils and toss to mix. Add ½ cup of the reserved lentil cooking liquid along with the fresh chopped thyme and rosemary and simmer until the lentil mixture begins to thicken. Adjust the seasoning and keep warm until duck is seared.

For the duck and sauce: preheat oven to 425°F. Score the fat side of the breasts in a crisscross pattern with a sharp knife. Add 1 tablespoon of olive oil to a hot sauté pan, season the breasts with salt and pepper, and sear them fat side down. When fat is brown and crispy, turn and sear the flesh side 1 minute. Set aside, covered.

Put the port in a small sauce pan and reduce by half until syrupy. In another sauce pan, sauté the shallots over low in 1 tablespoon of olive oil until translucent then add the cherries and port. Bring to a simmer, then reduce heat, whisking in butter off the heat. Adjust salt and pepper and keep warm.

Put the duck breasts skin side up on a rack over a roasting pan and then into the hot oven for about 8 minutes for medium, less for rare. Slice each on the bias into ½" slices. To serve, put the hot ragout on one side of the plates and fan the slices around it, spooning the sauce on top and garnishing if desired with roasted asparagus spears.

Serves 4

Ingredients

Lentils

1½ cups green lentils
4 cups chicken stock
1 sprig fresh thyme +1 teaspoon, chopped
1 sprig fresh rosemary +1 teaspoon, chopped
2 cloves garlic, peeled
4 slices applewood bacon, diced
1 tablespoon shallots, minced
½ cup reserved lentil cooking liquid
Salt and pepper

Duck and Sauce

4 8-ounce duck breasts, fat side scored
2 tablespoons olive oil
3 cups port wine
2 tablespoons shallots, minced
4 ounces dried sweet cherries
4 tablespoons butter
Salt and pepper

Seared Duck with Lentil Ragout and Dried Cherry Port Sauce

Above: Tuna Sashimi Salad

Like a simple Chicken Statler, which is an old-timey chophouse classic of nearly half a farm chicken. The Fishbones touch? "We brine it in maple syrup, brown sugar, and soy sauce with fresh herbs for a day or two, then, at service, we sear it off in a pan and finish it in the oven to crisp up the skin. We'll roast and purée butternut squash for a dressing—that's what we call stuffing in Maine. Add toasted, cubed garlic bread, a fresh herb or two, brown it up in the oven, then cover it with caramelized onion gravy, whew!"

"I'm pretty adamant about quality control in the kitchen," Paul insists, "but then, I can say to the sous chefs, what do you want to cook today? Go into the walk-in and get inspired, as long as it fits with what we're doing."

The result?

Paul says, "You can bring your *mémère*," — what Lewiston's numerous Franco-Americans call their grandmothers — "you can bring your foodie friends, and they're all going to find something to eat in a really comfortable place and not walk out feeling hungry or robbed."

Bourbon Walnut Tart with Chocolate Bits

Preheat oven to 350°F. Prepare enough of your favorite sugar crust recipe to line bottom and sides of an 11-inch tart pan with removable bottom. In a mixing bowl, cream together sugar, butter, and salt with the paddle attachment. When well mixed, blend in eggs, corn syrup, vanilla, and bourbon.

Line tart pan with prepared crust. Dot crust with walnuts and chocolate chips then pour filling over them until the syrup is just below the rim of the pan. Bake the tart on a sheet pan in case of overflow until firm to touch, 40-50 minutes.

Remove the tart from the pan. Serve warm with freshly whipped cream.

Serves 12

Ingredients

1 cup sugar
4 tablespoons unsalted butter
Pinch salt
5 eggs
14 ounces dark corn syrup
1 tablespoon vanilla
3 tablespoons bourbon whiskey
12 ounces pâte sucrée (sugar pastry crust)
1½ cups walnut halves
½ cup semi-sweet chocolate chips

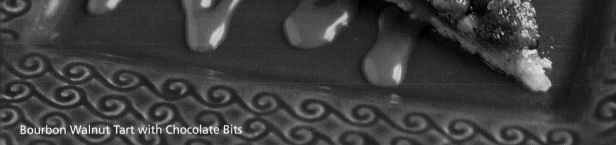

Bourbon Walnut Tart with Chocolate Bits

Francine Bistro

When so many working chefs describe the dream restaurant—and menu—they want to create "one day", what often comes out of their mouth is exactly the magical place Brian Hill has conjured up in Francine Bistro. In short: fresh-baked bread, one daily soup, four apps, four mains, three desserts, and a lovely, just-so wine list.

Oh, and one former punk rock star-turned-chef performing nightly without nets on a stage set of a kitchen for an audience occupying the 40-odd seats.

The short menu, Chef Hill says, "is just the most sensible thing to do in this intimate space, and it certainly reduces the anxiety around ordering. You're going to have the fish? Well, there it is, *the* fish. Still, I always try to be as ambitious as I can while building the menu around my own craving for luxury but also comfort. That gives us just enough room to use the incredible amount of fresh farm ingredients we get, and it almost makes each dish have more of a focus to it."

Wanting to hit that homey but rich note with a not-too-pricey fall dish, for example, he recently put together a local organic beef pot roast braised in cider. "Then local red kidney beans but super fancy," he recalls, "with orange and lemon zest, thyme, olive oil, and puréed so it's all velvety and red next to a cauliflower gratin using local cheese. All really simple, comforting food, but it has sense of luxuriousness about it."

Hill spent twelve years cooking in restaurants from New Orleans to New York and Boston. While he incorporates influences from all over, more often than not he returns to his roots as a farm boy from Warren. The last thing he wants to be, he says, "is a chef with a few tricks. It's great to learn the techniques, and we certainly use some of them here, but *you* have to make the food exciting, new. I can serve mashed turnips all winter long, but I better make them darned good mashed turnips."

As an avid fisherman particularly, Hill is a chef intensely aware of "the way the water smells here, the way the seafood smells. There are a lot of strong flavors in Maine seafood that match our *terroir*. Having caught a lot of cod, I know the way they smell, it's such a Maine thing. Mussels here smell like Maine seawater and our seaweed, our rocks and coast. It is such a responsibility not to screw that up. So, we'll make a *mouclade* of mussels where they are steamed open in dry apple cider and finished with egg yolks and cream and a little curry powder. Done right, that makes a great French dish—but it still tastes like Maine, like our waters."

And Hill doesn't make a big deal of the lengths he goes to when it comes to regional loyalty, whether it's that fish and shellfish, matsutake mushrooms, pea sprouts, or tomatoes. "My customers trust me," he says with a shrug. "They know they're getting the real thing. They can *taste* the quality of ingredients, and why else would I be cooking with it, anyway?"

Chef Brian Hill

Chef Hill at a Glance

Do you have any chef heroes?

Todd English, who I started out baking bread for, Susur Lee, David Chang.

When you're not cooking, what do you do to relax?

I have a horrible fishing addiction. It's getting bad.

Is there a particular spice mixture you like to play with?

I have a pretty bad fennel seed problem as well as my fishing problem.

Is there a country you like to travel to?

Mexico and Sicily are my two favorite places on earth—and I can eat and surf!

What's your favorite midnight snack?

Pasta cacio e pepe—with black pepper, pecorino, parmesan, and olive oil.

Chicken Liver Salad with Candied Bacon and Prunes

Prepare the bacon: put all ingredients in a shallow sauté pan and simmer very slowly until the water has evaporated and bacon is caramelized, about 10 minutes.

For the livers: heat a 10-inch skillet over high heat until thoroughly hot. Clean livers of any blood and veins, season with salt and pepper. Plump prunes 5 minutes in one cup boiling water. Put the butter, shallots, garlic, and rosemary in the hot pan together with the livers. When the livers are browned and caramelized on one side, turn with a long-handled fork. Watch out: chicken livers like to explode and spit at you! Add the prunes, balsamic vinegar, Cognac, and chicken stock. Peel the orange and make supremes of the segments.

(See epicurious.com for a good demonstration of supreme preparation.)

Keeping the livers over high heat, mash the prunes a little with the fork, and baste the livers frequently until the pan liquid is reduced to beautiful dark sauce. Season with sea salt and pepper.

Divide the frisée between four big plates, and spoon everything over the frisée while still very warm, garnish with the orange segments, radishes, candied bacon, and tarragon leaves. Season with good olive oil and a strong squeeze of lemon.

Below: Chicken Liver Salad with Candied Bacon and Prunes

Serves 4

Ingredients

Candied Bacon
4 ounces slab bacon cut in ½ inch dice
1 cup (8 ounces) water
½ teaspoon fennel seed
½ teaspoon coriander seed
¼ teaspoon chili flakes
2 tablespoons sugar

Chicken Livers
2 whole chicken livers, about 4 ounces
2 ounces butter
1 shallot, minced
1 clove garlic, minced
1½ tablespoons balsamic vinegar
4 prunes
1 teaspoon rosemary chopped
1 splash Cognac
½ cup chicken stock
1 blood orange
2 radishes, quartered
1 tablespoon fresh tarragon leaves
½ lemon
Olive oil
1 cup frisée or spinach, cleaned
Salt and pepper

"There are a lot of strong flavors in Maine seafood that match our terrior."

Pine Needle Mussels being prepared and ready to eat

Happy Joy Chicken Over Corn Purée

Preheat oven to 500°F. Pat chicken dry. Brush mushrooms clean of any dirt or leaves or centipedes. (You can use rehydrated dried mushrooms squeezed dry, too—black trumpet, porcini, chanterelles.)

Season bird inside and out with sea salt and pepper and stuff body cavity with thyme.

With your hand, carefully loosen the skin on the breast of the chicken and push the mushrooms under the skin on both sides of the breast. Cut a ½" slit in the flap of skin below each of the legs then cross the legs, tucking the end of each drumstick into the opposite slit. This "self trusses" the bird, allowing it to cook nice and evenly.

Place in a 10-inch skillet, sprinkle with a little more sea salt, and pop the pan into the very back of the oven and roast for 35 minutes.

While the chicken cooks, prepare the corn purée. Sweat garlic, shallots or onion, Herbes de Provence, and curry powder in the butter until soft. Add the wine and reduce. Add the corn kernels and cream and cook for 5 minutes. Blend thoroughly at high speed 3 minutes, then strain through a fine mesh sieve and season with sea salt and honey.

Take the chicken out of the oven, and let it rest for 10 minutes. Put the pan over moderate heat on top of the stove. Add one ounce butter to the skillet. Once the butter starts to foam use a spoon to baste the happy little chicken. Carve the chicken. Serve on the corn puree, garnishing with cracked black pepper.

Serves 4

Ingredients

Chicken
1 3½ pound natural corn fed chicken
1 whole bunch thyme, bruised slightly with your hands to release aroma
Sea salt, cracked pepper
1 ounce black trumpet mushrooms
1 ounce butter

Corn Purée
3 cups corn kernels (6 ears)
2 garlic cloves-sliced or minced
3 shallots or 1 Vidalia onion sliced
½ teaspoon Herbes de Provence
2 ounces butter
¼ cup Reisling or Pinot Gris
½ teaspoon curry powder
1½ cup cream

Happy Joy Chicken over Corn Purée

Northern Maine

Mount Desert Island

Above: Chefs James and Elizabeth Lindquist - Red Sky Restaurant
Below: Chef Maureen Cosgrove - Town Hill Bistro

Above: Chef Kyle Yarborough - Mache Bistro
Below: Chef Aaron Horvath - Havana Restaurant

Red Sky Restaurant

When James Lindquist was working at a Bar Harbor restaurant some years ago, his boss made the mistake of giving him three months off in the winter. By the spring, James and his wife, Elizabeth, along with James' niece, Erika, had opened Red Sky, nestled just off the main street of Southwest Harbor.

That was seven years ago, and they've never looked back.

"I'm the ninth out of ten kids," James explains, "and I spent a lot of time in the kitchen helping my mother. I remember sitting on the counter turning the handle of the meat grinder to make spaghetti sauce at the age of four or five. My approach to food comes from the family dinner table. Ours is the last generation to have had dinner together at the table every night. I grew up understanding that simple ingredients carefully prepared are the basis for really good food."

The Red Sky menu is a gentle reminder that, if you begin with a superior ingredient from not too far away, there is no need to overcomplicate your preparations. There, you will find Maine beef and poultry, North Atlantic fish like sand dabs, gray and lemon sole, Gulf of Maine shrimp and scallops, halibut and cod, each in its season and delivered direct from local purveyors like the Port Clyde Fresh Catch fishermen's cooperative. You will not find farmed jumbo shrimp or fish Fed-Exed from God-knows-where.

"Flying fish? That's unnatural," James says plainly, "so we stay local. Yes, it limits our selection some, but that's all right. What we have here is of the highest quality."

Chefs James and Elizabeth Lindquist

Chef Lindquist at a Glance

Where do you find your inspiration?

Walking in the woods.

What's your favorite cheese?

Really old cloth-bound cheddar, the sharper the better.

Do you have any chef heroes?

The chef at the taco stand on St. John.

Do you have a spice or flavor combination that pleases you?

Cayenne and cumin and thyme, like on our cocktail nuts.

Is there a book that has inspired you recently?

Heat by Bill Buford. Jeffrey Steingarten's books.

> **My approach to food comes from the family dinner table. Ours is the last generation to have had dinner together at the table every night. I grew up understanding that simple ingredients carefully prepared are the basis for really good food.**

Cod with Sautéed Kale, Bacon and Triple Citrus Beurre Blanc

For the beurre blanc: in a small saucepan sauté shallots in the clarified butter over medium heat until clear and soft but not browned, adding peppercorns, salt, and ground pepper. Add the zests, then the juices and wine, and simmer down until the sauce is the consistency of syrup. Pick out peppercorns. Remove sauce from heat and whisk in the chunks of cold butter, returning pan to low heat as necessary to melt butter. Sauce should be kept warm, but not over direct heat. Note: Reduction can be made ahead of time and butter whisked in up to 30 minutes before serving.

For the cod and kale garnish: preheat oven to 450°F. Prepare kale: remove tough center rib and cut each leaf into 3-4" wide pieces. Prepare a large bowl of ice water and a pot of boiling water. Put kale in boiling water for 30 seconds, drain, and submerge in ice water. When kale is cool, drain, squeeze out excess liquid, and set aside.

Combine flour, salt, and pepper in a shallow bowl and dredge each cod fillet. Heat clarified butter in a large skillet on high, and, when pan is very hot, add fillets and lightly brown each side, about 2 minutes. Transfer fish to a sheet pan and put in preheated oven for 8-10 minutes, until the flakes begin to separate. Reheat bacon in the same pan with the fish during the last 2 minutes of cooking.

As cod cooks, sauté the kale: melt the cold butter in a large skillet over high heat, add kale, toss, add a splash of white wine and a dash of salt and pepper, toss again.

To serve: place sautéed kale on plate, then a slice of bacon on top of the kale, then cod fillet on top of the bacon. Spoon beurre blanc over the fish, sprinkle with bread crumbs mixed with the chopped parsley and a pinch of salt and pepper, and serve immediately.

Serves 4

Ingredients

Beurre Blanc
1 tablespoon lemon zest
1 tablespoon lime zest
1 tablespoon orange zest
1 ounce fresh squeezed lemon juice
1 ounce fresh squeezed lime juice
1 ounce fresh squeezed orange juice
3 ounces dry white wine
3 whole black peppercorns
2 tablespoons finely chopped shallot
2 tablespoons clarified butter
4 ounces cold butter cut into ½" cubes
Salt and pepper to taste

Cod and Garnish
4 6-ounce Atlantic cod fillets
1 cup flour
1 teaspoon salt
¼ teaspoon ground black pepper
2 tablespoons clarified butter
1 tablespoon cold butter
1 bunch kale, rinsed
Splash dry white wine
4 strips Sunset Acres bacon, cooked crisp
½ cup bread crumbs
3 tablespoons chopped parsley

North Atlantic Cod with Sautéed Kale, Bacon and Triple Citrus Beurre Blanc

Above: Lemon Custard

What you also have is serendipity, a forager walking in with chanterelle mushrooms at noon, just as James is scratching his head to come up with a sauce for Elizabeth's linguini.

"I make the pasta fresh every day," Elizabeth explains, "and James has rigged up a whole system of dowels and barstools so, sometimes, if you stop by in the afternoon, all you see is beet tagliatelli hanging everywhere to dry."

There is also James' bread, baked fresh each morning.

And their desserts: "We lean towards the simple," James says, "like gingerbread topped with caramel sauce and cream whipped with a little applejack."

"He always said he would do anything in the restaurant but the baking." Elizabeth finishes, laughing. "Now he does it three hours a day and still, we can't keep up. If the customers had their way, we'd have ten desserts on the menu."

Tagliatelle with Spinach, Baby Beets, and Goat Cheese

Do ahead: put the beets in a roasting pan and brush with olive oil. Sprinkle with salt and roast in a 375°F oven for 45 minutes to 1 hour depending on the size of the beets. When done, a knife should go through them with no resistance. Trim beet ends, peel beets while warm, and slice into wedges.

Preheat oven to 375°F. Put large pot of water on to boil for the pasta. Form goat cheese into 1 ounce buttons and coat in bread crumbs (or chopped toasted nuts or sesame seeds, if preferred). Put goat cheese buttons in heated oven, and check in two minutes. Crust should brown and cheese should soften but still hold its shape.

While the pasta is cooking, wrap the beet wedges in foil and put them in the oven to warm, then make the sauce. In a large skillet, sauté shallots in the butter over medium high heat until translucent, adding salt and pepper. Add thyme leaves and cook 1 minute. Add lemon juice and wine, lower heat, and reduce liquid by half. When liquid is reduced, whisk in 1 or 2 tablespoons of water from the pasta pot. Drain pasta and toss noodles in the sauce with roasted beets and spinach.

Transfer to 4 pasta bowls and serve topped with the toasted cheese buttons.

Serves 4

Ingredients

Pasta and Garnish

1 pound fresh tagliatelle, preferably beet
2 dozen baby beets
½ cup olive oil
Salt
1 pound fresh baby spinach, twice-washed
4 ounces chèvre-style goat cheese
1 cup fresh bread crumbs

Thyme, Butter and Lemon Sauce

2 tablespoons finely chopped shallot
Pinch of coarse salt
¼ teaspoon black pepper
1 tablespoon fresh thyme leaves
1 ounce fresh lemon juice
4 ounces dry white wine
2 ounces cold unsalted butter in cubes
2 tablespoons of pasta water (adjust with more if desired)

Tagliatelle with Fresh Spinach, Roasted Baby Beets, and Goat Cheese

Town Hill Bistro

Talk to many unenlightened chefs in southern Maine—Portland, say, and they will complain about being on the wrong end of the East Coast supply chain that brings many specialty products north out of Boston, New York, and points south. Talk to Maureen Cosgrove, chef/owner of Town Hill Bistro outside Bar Harbor, and she talks

about being on the wrong end of the supply chain stretching up from, well, Portland. Far from settling for less choice, she has made a virtue out of necessity by developing a loyal group of very local suppliers and drawing on twenty years of cooking and baking to provide a cuisine that springs from the traditions of her region and, naturally, uses its riches to the fullest.

"It's how I started cooking," she says, "as the oldest daughter in a Boston Irish-Catholic family with four kids. Even as a teenager, I liked to cook, and, once the family found out I could cook, I was doomed."

Today, this resourcefulness adds a particular zing and spontaneity to her dishes unusual in these parts. "My bartender has a day job," she jokes. "She's a sternman on a lobsterboat. So she walks in at 4pm every day with halibut, lobster, crab. There's a new Dutch-style mussel farm outside the Bay, and we get them delivered twice a week by the son of the owner. All our food scraps go to a man who raises pigs. In the fall after butchering, he'll just show up. We only get the shanks, the fatback, and the belly—because those cuts have more flavor. At the farmers' market twice a week, I get yelled at by old ladies because I'll fill four big fish tubs full of vegetables. Then, the farmers stop by here on their way out of town with their surplus, and I'll take everything on a truck. Three days later, it's all gone."

The single-sheet menu changes so frequently, she says, because she gets bored and an opportunity presents itself. "Sometimes we'll start making sushi and, before we know it, we're having Asian week." She says, laughing. "But then, too, we're not afraid to try some very traditional, if unusual, New England dishes." Like? "We had 30 orders of beef marrow bones specially cut for us one week this fall. We roasted them and served the plate with toast and a salad of parsley and preserved lemon because the marrow is so unctuous and rich that it needs a citrus to cut it. People were sucking it out of the bones!" They sold out in two nights.

Sous Chef Michelle Campbell

Chef Cosgrove at a Glance

Where do you find your inspiration?

Raw ingredients, having to work with what's in front of me.

Do you have any chef heroes?

No, but the woman at the coffee shop makes a great breakfast sandwich.

Do you have a spice or a flavor that pleases you?

Allspice, cinnamon, nutmeg but also Asian/Indian spicy stuff.

What do you do to relax?

I like to be outside, in nature, with my son.

What's your favorite cheese?

Any Hahn's End. And I love Silvery Moon Camembert.

Maine Shrimp and Peaky-Toe Crab Salad

For the vinaigrette: combine first 5 ingredients in the bowl of a blender or Cuisanart and blend well. Slowly drizzle oil in while blending. Chill.

For the salad: with a sharp paring knife, remove all skin and pith from fruits. "Supreme" the fruit by cutting segments out using sharp knife. (Go to epicurious.com for a demonstration video.) In a large bowl, combine citrus, shrimp, crab, chives and about half of vinaigrette. Toss well to combine. Portion microgreens evenly in shallow serving bowls. Place equal amounts of seafood mixture on top of microgreens. Top with remaining dressing if desired. Serve at once.

Note: Though Maine shrimp are available unpeeled, buying them peeled (and cooked), saves you time. The best Maine crabmeat for this salad is Peaky-Toe, which is only sold pre-cooked.

Serves 4-6 as a first course

Ingredients

Juice of 1 lemon
1¼ teaspoon salt
1 egg yolk
1½ teaspoon sugar
1 tablespoon white wine vinegar
¾ cup canola oil
1 tablespoon chopped fresh chives
2 cups microgreens
8 ounces peeled, cooked Maine shrimp (see note)
8 ounces Maine crabmeat (see note)
1 grapefruit
2 navel oranges

Maine Shrimp and Peaky-Toe Crab Salad

> *Cosgrove is thoughtful about her cooking, seeking to hit the perfect balance of casual, good, and local at an affordable price no matter the season.*

Chef/owner Maureen Cosgrove, right, and her partner, JJ Zeph, left.

Handmade Rustic Gnocchi with Winter Sauce

Make the gnocchi: peel and quarter potatoes. Boil them in salted water until tender, 10-12 minutes, then drain and put through a ricer. (Or mash them with a fork on a clean towel). Spread them onto a clean work surface, sprinkle them with sea salt and 1½ cup of the flour. Knead mixture together with your hands until a slightly sticky ball can be formed.

Portion mixture into 4 pieces and, using the palms of your hands, form each piece into a snake about 1" in diameter and 1 foot long. You may need to sprinkle dough occasionally with remaining flour. Cut each snake into pieces 1" long.

To cook: brush the olive oil onto a clean cookie sheet. Using a slotted spoon, transfer gnocchi pieces into a pot of simmering water. When gnocchi pop up and float to the surface (about 2-3 minutes), transfer them to the cookie sheet using the slotted spoon and agitate sheet to coat lightly with olive oil. Let cool. At this point, the gnocchi can be covered and refrigerated for up to 2 days.

Pan fry gnocchi in 2 tablespoons olive oil (or butter) in a skillet on medium high, turning to brown each side. They are now ready to serve with your favorite sauce.

Sauce: Heat skillet to medium high and add olive oil. Add mushrooms and sauté for 2 minutes. Add spinach and sauté 2 minutes more. Add stock, heavy cream, cheese, and pepper and reduce for about 2 minutes. Add bacon and portion sauce between serving plates.

Top with pan-fried gnocchi, and serve at once.

Serves 4 as entrée / 6-8 as first course

Ingredients
Gnocchi
2 large russet potatoes
1 teaspoon fine sea salt
2 cups all purpose flour
2 tablespoons olive oil or butter

Sauce
4 slices thick bacon, crumbled after cooking
2 cups sliced mushrooms, your choice
2 cups spinach or pea shoots
½ cup grated hard cheese*
½ cup chicken or vegetable stock
½ cup heavy cream
½ teaspoon ground black pepper
2 tablespoons olive oil

*Cheese: we like Seal Cove Farm Olga, but Parmesan works well, too.

Handmade Rustic Gnocchi with Winter Sauce

Cosgrove, an energetic redhead who never seems to stop moving, is also thoughtful about her cooking, seeking to hit the perfect balance of casual, good, and local at an affordable price no matter the season. August's poached lobster with a warm citrusy gin-lemonade dressing over mixed greens gives way to December's braised pork shank with garlic mash or polenta. "I'm always asking myself, what do I want to eat in the summer? Winter? We let our instincts guide us."

"Us" is, along with a small staff, her partner, JJ Zeph, who runs the front of the house but is equally adept at turning his hand to other kitchen tasks as needed. "JJ works really hard." Maureen says. "He'll break down a case of ducks while I take our son swimming in the afternoon, then he has to work the house for six hours."

And the "house" is actually two houses joined by a wide passageway, one the post-and-beam dining room, the other an extended kitchen. Everywhere, there are touches of the handmade, unique and unusual wood- and metalwork, fixtures, and glass. "All of the work in here was done by local artists. One friend built the bar; another did a lot of the woodwork. We wouldn't have such a nice place if we didn't have a lot of friends who brought their talents to making the whole place what it is. We support them, and they support us."

Because Town Hill is not in downtown Bar Harbor, their clientele is a bit different than the norm. 'Here, we survive thanks to the local community, and it's great in the summer when tourists find us, though we can't rely on them. We also have a lot of single diners here, and they don't feel intimidated. We don't have any wine that's $12 a glass, or any $40 entrées. And the fishermen love to come here even if they're just having a martini and a steak at the bar."

"I think," she finishes thoughtfully, "that you need to know who you are. We work harder than most people to make this the kind of place where lots of folks like to come and feel, well, at home!"

Does it get any simpler than that?

Simple Tiramisù

At Town Hill Bistro, we serve this with different whipped creams and other toppings depending on the season, fresh berries in summer and housemade cookies in the colder months, for example.

In mixer, whip together mascarpone, heavy cream, vanilla, and confectioners sugar.

Combine coffee and Kahlua and let cool slightly. Dip ladyfingers into coffee mixture and lay snuggly in the bottom of a 9" x 12" brownie pan. On top of the ladyfingers, spread half of the cream mixture and smooth. Repeat with more layers of coffee-dipped ladyfingers and cream until they fill the pan. Sift cocoa on top of last layer of cream and refrigerate for at least 3 hours. Cut into squares to serve.

9-12 servings

Ingredients

48 toasted ladyfingers
16 ounces mascarpone cheese
2 cups heavy cream
1 teaspoon vanilla
½ cup confectioners sugar
6 cups strong fresh brewed coffee
¾ cup Kahlua
½ cup dark cocoa powder

Mache Bistro

If the vast state of Maine can be said to have restaurant micro-climates, none is more rarified than Mount Desert Island. Just ask Kyle and Marie Yarborough, whose Mache Bistro in downtown Bar Harbor seems to operate only at two speeds, busy and busier. In an intimate setting with creaky floors, an elbow-worn bar in one corner,

and seats for fewer than 40 diners in the rest of the space, summer's visitors mean no days off from June through October, with winter a welcome respite when the locals crowd the tables.

Having such a diverse clientele "makes you a better cook, definitely," Kyle says. "People here are so aware of what they're eating, and they don't want to go to a so-called 'tourist' restaurant. That's fine with us, because what we offer is traditional bistro style cuisine—simple, quality ingredients, prepared with traditional, simple techniques."

"But unlike 90% of the restaurants on the island, we do stay open year-round," Marie says, "and the other side of that is, most of the time, we really are cooking for the locals. Kyle's happy because he has so much more creative freedom in the kitchen *because* our friends and neighbors are so open-minded and trust us."

So if you're imagining gussied up burgers with a side of mac 'n cheese or steak frites, think again. Some of these locals are scallop divers and halibut fishermen who come by to see what he does with the seafood they offer him. His relationships with them are so precious, he points out, because most of their catch is bound for Portland, Boston, and New York before anyone else knows it has been landed. "If they don't know you," he puts it, "they don't call you, and you don't get those scallops so fresh they're still quivering."

"And how can you say no to a 60-pound line-caught halibut when the guy tells you he's just coming into the harbor and so he might be a few minutes?" Kyle asks, chuckling, even though it means he'll have to call another chef down the road to share the harvest with—"and then come up with a 5-course halibut tasting menu, quick!" he jokes.

"*French Flavors, Local Flair*" is Mache's motto, and their one-page menu, which changes almost every day, has ample evidence of that, from winter's cassoulets and braises, to lighter fish dishes and lashings of seasonal produce at its peak built into intricate salads in warmer months.

Along with its appealingly unpretentious food, Mache has a reputation of being a place where you might run into just about anyone. "In summer season, we might have a whole room of foreign languages," Kyle says, "and New Yorkers complimenting us on their meals."

"That is definitely the summer," Marie adds, laughing. "Other times of the year we stick our head out of the kitchen and see the farmer perched on a stool next to the fisherman, one tucking into the seared cod and the other the braised lamb shanks, and we can only wonder what they're talking about."

Chef Kyle Yarborough

Chef Yarborough at a Glance

Where do you find your inspiration?

In the unusual and fresh things that come to my door, and in traveling.

Do you have any chef heroes?

Norman Van Aken for his New World/Latin/Fusion cooking.

Do you have a spice or a flavor that pleases you?

Ancho chili. It has a deep, earthy, smoky flavor without too much heat.

Is there a book that has inspired you recently?

Culinary Artistry by Andrew Dornenburg and Karen Page.

What country do you think has the most underrated food?

Mexico and its traditional food, authentic Oaxacan specifically.

Grilled Hanger Steak with Blue Cheese Butter

For the blue cheese butter: place butter, crumbled blue cheese, garlic salt, olive oil, and chopped parsley in a medium bowl. Mix well to combine flavors. Turn out onto a sheet of waxed paper. Shape into a log, then roll it up in the waxed paper. Refrigerate until needed.

For the steaks: drizzle steaks with olive oil, then rub with crushed garlic. Combine black pepper, garlic salt, salt, thyme, and rosemary in a small bowl to make a rub and season steaks generously with it, pressing it onto both sides. Put steaks on a platter, cover, and let them rest for 30 minutes to 1 hour, refrigerated.

Turn grill to high, or heat a cast iron or other heavy skillet over high heat. Sear steaks on the hot grill or in the skillet until a crust has formed, about 4 to 5 minutes. Turn the steaks and either move them to a cooler part of the grill, or reduce heat to medium, and cook to medium rare, about 4 to 5 minutes. Set the steaks aside to rest for 2 to 3 minutes. Then, slice steak into 5 or 6 medallions. Slice a walnut-sized chunk of blue cheese butter from the log and place on top of the sliced steak. Serve over mashed potatoes or creamy polenta. Blue cheese log will freeze for up to a month. You can substitute New York strip or skirt steak for hanger.

Serves 4

Ingredients

Blue Cheese Butter
4 ounces unsalted butter at room temperature
2 ounces blue cheese, crumbled (Maytag or your local favorite)
¼ teaspoon garlic salt
1 teaspoon good quality olive oil
2 tablespoons fresh parsley, chopped

Steak
3 tablespoons coarsely ground black pepper
½ teaspoon garlic salt
½ teaspoon salt
½ teaspoon thyme
½ teaspoon rosemary, chopped
4 6-ounce hanger steaks
2 cloves garlic, peeled and crushed
2 tablespoons olive oil

Grilled Hanger Steak with Blue Cheese Butter

People here are so aware of what they're eating, and they don't want to go to a so-called 'tourist' restaurant. That's fine with us, because what we offer is traditional bistro style cuisine . . . **"**

Chocolate Pot de Crème with Ancho Chili

Cabernet Poached Pears Stuffed with Cranberry Blue Cheese

Two crisp, minerally whites that we serve with this are a Pierre Boniface Âpremont Vin de Savoie, 2007, or a Joseph Drouhin Saint-Veran Chardonnay, 2007.

Preheat oven to 350°F. Halve pears and place in a baking dish flesh side down together with wine, vinegar, brown sugar, salt, and honey. Cover with foil, and bake for 1 hour. Allow pears to cool in liquid. Scoop out and discard pear cores and seeds to create a space for the filling. Reserve cooking liquid.

While pears cook, in a mixer fitted with a paddle attachment blend cream cheese, mayonnaise, olive oil, 2 ounces blue cheese, ¼ cup pecans and ¼ cup dried cranberries until well incorporated.

Divide filling into 4 parts and fill each pear half. Toss arugula with olive oil and divide among four plates. Place stuffed pear on top of arugula and garnish with reserved pecans, cranberries, and blue cheese. Drizzle reserved cooking liquid over pear and greens.

serves 4

Ingredients

Pears
2 Bosch Pears
½ cup Cabernet Sauvignon
¼ cup balsamic vinegar
2 tablespoons brown sugar
½ teaspoon salt
1 tablespoon honey
3 cups baby arugula
2 tablespoons olive oil

Blue Cheese Filling
¼ cup chopped pecans, plus
    1 tablespoon for garnish
¼ cup dried cranberries, plus
    1 tablespoon for garnish
3 ounces cream cheese (room temperature)
1 tablespoon mayonnaise
1 tablespoon olive oil
2 ounces blue cheese, plus 1 ounce for
    garnish (Maytag or your local favorite)

Cabernet Poached Pears Stuffed with Cranberry Blue Cheese

Havana Restaurant

When Michael Boland and Deirdre Swords opened Havana Restaurant in downtown Bar Harbor in 1999, the couple's inspiration was not some whimsical imagined association with tropical climes. Rather, the two had spent every winter of the previous decade traveling, living—and eating—in different South and Central American

and Afro-Caribbean landscapes. The restaurant became, then, a place to make those remembered tastes come alive, albeit with the additional accents of Maine and its corner of the Atlantic, this marriage of influences coloring everything from the unique menu to the bright décor and warm welcome, even to the cocktails offered at the bar.

"A *tres leches* cake from Nicaragua, moist and dense with *dulce de leche*," Boland recalls, almost licking his lips at the memory, "or a *moqueca* in Bahia, on the coast of Brazil. That's a stew made with *dende* oil, a really rich palm oil, and whatever seafood they have available. Here, we use Maine shrimp and mussels and, of course, lobster. It is one of our favorites, and our customers', because it makes that direct connection between what we have here and what we ate there."

Though Havana's plates come spiced with ethnic and cultural stories from the couple's travels, stories they often find themselves telling their customers, they take their commitment to the authenticity of the food very seriously.

"Though I spend half my time in the kitchen and have a hand in developing every recipe, I am not a chef," Michael states plainly, "so it is very important that we help the staff share our vision so that it gets translated to the plate." So important, in fact, that they have begun to send part of the Havana team each winter to Brazil and other southern destinations for a few weeks, to breathe in firsthand the life there. "There's nothing to compare to being there, shopping in the markets, cooking with the ingredients, eating the food yourself at a street stall or in a humble restaurant – and then being able to come back with these new ideas and experiences that they then make their own."

One of the couple's favorite corners of South America is the three Guyanas, British, Dutch, and French, in the northeast of the continent. "The British brought slaves," Michael says, "who brought their West African staples, then they brought the Indians in, with their spices and cuisine. Right next door is Dutch Guyana, and they brought the Javans in from Indonesia. In the Surinam jungle you come on a village and everyone's speaking Dutch creole but eating all kinds of Javanese food—in South America!"

Which is why, on the Havana menu you'll find the Indian roti flatbread topped with an island chutney, or a duck confit with *pilpil*, the Guyanese hot pepper relish, or a fish curry playing that sweet/savory/spicy Indonesian song. A more Latin influence comes in dishes like a duck empanada, flaky pastry filled with shredded pulled duck seasoned with 5-Spice powder and sauced with a cilantro/orange pesto.

Chef Aaron Horvath

Chef Horvath at a Glance

Where do you find your inspiration?

In what my purveyors bring to the door, new or old.

Do you have any chef heroes?

I pay attention to the big guys, but I try not to let them influence me too much.

Do you have a spice or a flavor that pleases you?

Fresh organic hot peppers kept as raw and sweet as possible.

Do you have a favorite cheese?

Roaring 40s Blue Cheese, from King's Island near Tasmania.

Do you have a kitchen utensil that is particularly pleasing to you?

My blades, my Japanese folded-steel blades.

Cranberry & Chorizo Stuffed Pork Tenderloin

For the pork tenderloin: preheat oven to 350°F. Ask your butcher to butterfly the tenderloin for you. Otherwise, slice the loin lengthwise halfway through, open the two flaps like a book, and pound them flat with a meat tenderizer so the whole tenderloin is more or less of the same thickness.

For the cranberry and chorizo stuffing: in a large heavy pan sauté the sausage and drain off excess fat. Over medium heat add onion, the three peppers, garlic, cumin, and cranberries. Cook until the onions are translucent but not browned. Add crushed tortillas, chicken broth and tomato paste. Cook for 1 minute. Add all fresh herbs. Remove from the heat.

Place the stuffing in the middle of the pork tenderloin. Roll the tenderloin around the stuffing, then tie the roll with loops of butcher's twine. Heat a sauté pan on high with 2 tablespoons of oil. Sear the outside of the pork tenderloin till golden brown. Place in the preheated oven for 15 minutes, slice, and serve. At Havana, we garnish this with a bright, wilted green like spinach or chard and accompany it with wasabi mashed potatoes.

Serves 4

Ingredients

2 pounds pork tenderloin, butterflied
1 tablespoon ground cumin
1½ cups frozen cranberries
1 yellow pepper, diced
1 green pepper, diced
1 red pepper, diced
4 garlic cloves, cleaned and minced
2 teaspoons fresh oregano, chopped
2 teaspoons fresh thyme, chopped
2 teaspoons fresh parsley, chopped
1 Spanish onion, diced
8 ounces chicken broth
⅓ cup tomato paste
½ pound chorizo
½ pound tortilla chips, crumbled

Cranberry & Chorizo Stuffed Pork Tenderloin

Chef Aaron Horvath Plating Seafood Paella

Blueberry Glazed Seared Duck over Sweet Potato Purée

Heat the onions and jalapeño in 1 tablespoon of the oil in a large, heavy-bottomed saucepan until translucent but not browned, about 5 minutes, then add the garlic and blueberries. Cook until the blueberries release most of their liquid then add brown sugar. Stir until the sugar is incorporated and continue simmering the sauce until it is syrupy.

Peel and cube the potatoes, then boil in plenty of water until soft. Purée in a mixer together with the sour cream, butter, and salt and pepper to taste. Keep warm.

In a large sauté pan heat the remaining tablespoon oil. Crosshatch the skin side of each duck breast, taking care not to slice down to the flesh. Sear the breasts in the hot pan skin side down until browned, flip, cooking about 3 minutes per side for medium doneness. Remove from heat and let rest 4 minutes before slicing into ½" medallions against the grain. Place a dollop of potato purée onto four serving plates, fan duck breast slices, then top with the blueberry sauce.

Serves 4

Ingredients

4 6-ounce duck breasts
2 tablespoons canola oil
3 cups Maine blueberries
2 Spanish onions
2 jalapeños, seeded and diced
3 garlic cloves, diced
1 cup brown sugar
4 large sweet potatoes
1 cup sour cream
1 tablespoon butter
Salt and pepper to taste

Blueberry Glazed Seared Duck over Sweet Potato Purée

Aaron Horvath, Havana's chef de cuisine of five years, takes an almost Method Acting approach to translating the couple's ideas to the plate. "First, I'll research the culture and its food." He explains. "Why do they use this starch and these techniques and this kind of pepper or fresh herb? Then I'll master that technique, cooking it and creating it over and over, getting all the flavors right and how to infuse them and make them work off each other. Then, I can begin to play, but not too much."

And though some seasons impose their limits, much of the year, Horvath says, "my walk-in is 70-80% local and organic, the fish and shellfish is from our ocean backyard, and we are taking from the state and the region as much as we possibly can."

Boland, a serial restaurateur who with his wife also owns the Rupununi Bar & Grill up the street and has recently opened Havana South on Portland's Wharf Street, seems to have the urge to feed people in his blood.

Havana Restaurant's Colorful Décor

"I love feeding people." He says. "It really is one of the most intimate things you can do. What charges me up in making a restaurant, which you have to do all over again every night, by the way, is the creativity that you get to express. And not just in the dishes themselves, but in the whole creation of a space, of a feel, of a vibe, of the menus, the floor plan, the feng shui of it."

Sustainability and green thinking are also things Boland takes far beyond lip service. Two of his restaurants use solar-powered hot water and were the first in Maine to be certified by Dine Green for environmental practices they continue today. "For us," he says, "it is not a new story but something integral to everything we do. The sustainability of our restaurants only begins with the local produce and seafood the diner finds on the table."

Though Havana's plates come spiced with ethnic and cultural stories from the couple's travels, stories they often find themselves telling their customers, they take their commitment to the authenticity of the food very seriously.

Coconut Crusted Tuna with Plum/Chili Jam and Black Rice

Mix the farofa or matzo and coconut in a bowl and set aside. In a small saucepan, bring the water, soy sauce, red pepper flakes, vinegar, sugar, and plums to a simmer and cook over low until plums have broken down. Strain out plum seeds and skins and keep sauce warm.

For the rice: bring 4 cups water to a boil, add rice, and return to boil. Reduce to simmer for 20 minutes. When still slightly al dente (black rice has more crunch than white rice), add sweet soy sauce, spinach, and the two juices. Keep warm.

For the tuna: heat the canola oil in a skillet large enough for all of the filets over high heat. Dredge the tuna pieces in the coconut mixture and sear until brown on each side, about one minute per side so that the steak is crusty on the outside and almost raw on the inside. Slice into ½" slices. Serve by dividing rice on 4 plates, topping with fanned tuna slices and plum sauce.

Serves 4

Ingredients

Tuna and jam:

4 5-ounce yellowfin tuna steaks*
1 teaspoon canola oil
¾ cup farofa (cassava flour)**
¾ cup toasted coconut flakes
4 ounces fresh plums
¼ cup soy sauce
1 teaspoon red pepper flakes
¼ cup red wine vinegar
2 cups water
1 cup sugar

Rice

2 cups Chinese black rice
4 cups water
4 tablespoons sweet soy sauce
2 cups baby spinach, well-rinsed
2 ounces fresh orange juice
2 ounces pineapple juice

*Ask your fishmonger for pole-caught sustainable yellowfin tuna.

**Matzo meal may be substituted.

Contacts and Opening Information

Anneke Jans Restaurant is at 60 Wallingford Square in Kittery, telephone 207-439-0001. Web: **www.annekejans.net.** Open year round for dinner at 5pm to close. Reservations call or through Open Table.

Azure Café is located at 123 Main Street in Freeport, telephone 207-865-1237. Visit us at **www.azurecafe.com**, e-mail us at info@azurecafe.com, and find us on Twitter at Azure Café and Facebook at Azure Café. We are open for lunch and dinner 7 days a week. Lunch 11:30am to 3pm, weekend light fare 3pm to 4pm, dinner Sunday to Thursday, 5 pm to 9pm, Friday and Saturday 5pm to 10 pm, closed Christmas and Thanksgiving Day.

Bar Lola is at 100 Congress Street in Portland, telephone 207-775-5652. Web: **www.barlola.net**, e-mail: info@barlola.net. Open year round Wednesday through Saturday 5pm to 10pm. Reservations also through Open Table.

Caiola's Restaurant is located at 58 Pine Street in Portland, telephone 207-772-1110. On the web: **www.caiolas.com**. We are closed Mondays, open 5pm to 9:30pm Tuesday through Thursday, 5pm to 10pm Friday and Saturday, Sunday brunch 9am to 2pm. Open year round, with private dining room and seasonal terrace.

Cinque Terre Restaurant is at 36 Wharf Street in Portland, telephone 207-347-6154. Visit us at **www.cinqueterremaine.com**, e-mail: reservations@cinqueterremaine.com, and find us on Facebook at Cinque Terre. Serving dinner nightly at 5pm.

El Camino Cantina is at 15 Cushing Street in Brunswick, telephone 207-725-8228. E-mail: elcaminocantina@hotmail.com. Open Tuesday through Thursday 5pm to 9pm, Friday and Saturday 5pm to 9:30pm. Open year round, closed Thanksgiving and one week at Christmas. We do not take reservations.

Fishbones American Grill is at 70 Lincoln Street in Lewiston, 207-333-3663. Web: **www.fishbonesmaine.com**, e-mail: gofish@fishbonesag.com. Open year round for lunch and dinner: Tuesday through Friday 11:30am to 9:30pm, Saturday 4pm to 9:30pm. Closed Thanksgiving and Christmas Day. Seasonal Sunday brunch September through Father's Day, 10am to 2pm.

five fifty five is at 555 Congress Street in Portland, telephone 207-761-0555. Web: **www.fivefifty-five.com**, e-mail through contact page on website. Open 7 days for dinner 5pm through 10:30pm, plus Sunday brunch 9:30am to 2pm. Open year round, closed Christmas day. Reservations also through Open Table.

Fore Street Restaurant is at 288 Fore Street in Portland, telephone 207-775-2717. Web: **www.forestreetrestaurant.com**. Open year round, Sunday through Thursday 5:30pm to 10pm, Friday and Saturday 5:30pm to 10:30pm (Sundays October through May, close at 9:30.) Bar opens at 5pm. Closed Thanksgiving Day, Christmas Eve and Christmas Day. We hold about one-third of our seats for walk-ins year round. We encourage reservations.

Francine Bistro is at 55 Chestnut Street in Camden, telephone 207-230-0083. On the web: **www.francinebistro.com**, e-mail: francinebistro@myfairpoint.net. We are open year round, Tuesday to Saturday for dinner from 5:30pm to 10pm, closed Christmas and Thanksgiving.

The **Harraseeket .Inn Maine Dining Room and Broad Arrow Tavern** are at 162 Main Street in Freeport, telephone 207-865-9377 or 800-342-6423. Web: **www.harraseeketinn.com**, e-mail: Harraseeke@aol.com. Open 7 days a week year round, 7am to 10pm, open all holidays and featuring wood-fired ovens, lunch buffet and Sunday brunch.

Havana Restaurant is at 318 Main Street in Bar Harbor, telephone: 207-288-CUBA. Web: **www.havanamaine.com**, e-mail: info@havanamaine.com. In season hours, May through November and mid-December through New Year's Eve, serving dinner 7 days at 5pm to close. Closed Christmas Eve and Christmas Day. We accommodate all food allegies and welcome large group reservations.

Hugo's Restaurant is at 88 Middle Street in Portland, telephone 207-774-8538. Web: **www.hugos.net**. Open year round, Tuesday through Thursday 5:30pm to 9pm, Friday and Saturday 5:30 to 9:30. Reservations by phone only.

Joshua's Restaurant is at 1637 US Route One (also called the Post Road), telephone 207-646-3355. Web: **www.joshuas.biz**. Open year round Monday through Saturday 5pm to 10pm. Closed Thanksgiving and Christmas Day, plus two annual vacations in early November and March (check website).

Mache Bistro is at 135 Cottage Street in Bar Harbor, telephone 207-288-0447. Web: **www.machebistro.com**, e-mail: info@machebistro.com. Visit us on Facebook at "Mache Bistro Bar Harbor Restaurant". Open April through February, Monday through Saturday, closed Thanksgiving Day and Christmas Day.

Old Port Sea Grill is at 93 Commercial Street in Portland, telephone 207-879-6100. Web: **www.theoldportseagrill.com**. Open 7 days a week, serving lunch and dinner from 11:30am to close. Reservations by phone and through Open Table. Features full raw bar and large lounge and bar area. Check website for holiday closings.

Red Sky Restaurant is at 14 Clark Point Road in the town of Southwest Harbor on Mount Desert Island, telephone 207-244-0476. Web: **www.redskyrestaurant.com**, e-mail: info@redskyrestaurant.com (but we do not take e-mail reservations); Facebook: Redskyrestaurant. Open 7 days in summer season 5:30pm to 9pm, Friday through Sunday winter. Open February through December, closed January.

Seagrass Bistro is located at 30 Forest Fall Drive in Yarmouth, telephone 207-846-3885. Web: **www.seagrassbistro.com**, e-mail: seagrassbistro@seagrassbistro.com. Open year round Wednesday through Saturday, serving from 5:30pm. Closed Christmas Day, New Year's Day, and Fourth of July.

Solo Bistro is located at 128 Front Street in Bath, telephone 207-443-3373. On the web: **www.solobistro.com**, e-mail: info@solobistro.com. We are open year round, 7 days a week in high season and Tuesday through Saturday the rest of the year. We serve dinner from 5pm to close, and are closed Thanksgiving, Christmas Eve, and Christmas.

Town Hill Bistro is on the corner of Crooked Road and Route 102, 1317 Route 102, Town Hill Bar Harbor, telephone 207-288-1011. On the web: **www.townhillbistro.com**, e-mail: townhillbistro@gmail.com, Facebook: Town Hill Bistro, blog: townhillbistro. wordpress.com. Summer hours open 7 days 5:30pm to close, winter hours Tuesday through Saturday, 5:30pm to close. Check website for yearly vacation closings.